# FIRST-TIME HOME BUYER

# FIRST-TIME HOME BUYER

### The COMPLETE GUIDE
### *to* AVOIDING ROOKIE MISTAKES

**SCOTT TRENCH AND MINDY JENSEN**

**BiggerPockets®**
PUBLISHING
Denver, Colorado

# Praise for
# *Set for Life* by Scott Trench

"[This] personally narrated audiobook is geared toward those of us at the start of our career journey for whom the end feels unimaginable. If you're worried about how you'll ever save enough to retire, settle down with Trench's calming voice and sage advice in *Set for Life*."

**—from Audible's "20 Best Finance Audiobooks for Amateurs and Masters Alike"**

"Cogently written and ideal for those beginning their careers who are not averse to risk; some may find this fiscal plan too audacious, but others will likely embrace its spirit and pursue it with fervor."

**—Kirkus Reviews**

"*Set for Life* provides a plan for your money in a no-nonsense way... If you take these ideas to heart, then you could completely transform the trajectory of your life."

**—Robert Farrington, Founder of The College Investor**

# Praise for
# *How to Sell Your Home*
# by Mindy Jensen

"There is so much that goes into this process and it can be very overwhelming for homeowners. Mindy does a phenomenal job of providing a comprehensive yet easy to digest A-to-Z guide for homeowners so that time and money can be saved. I enjoyed learning new strategies and I am looking forward to using these strategies on my next sale!"

**—Liz Faircloth, Co-founder of
The Real Estate InvestHER Community**

"A great read for both real estate investors and homeowners... It's critical to know the ins and outs of selling your home fast and at a high price, and Mindy does just that in *How to Sell Your Home*."

**—Andrew Syrios, BiggerPockets blog
author and real estate investor**

**First-Time Home Buyer: The Complete Playbook to Avoiding Rookie Mistakes**
Scott Trench and Mindy Jensen

Published by BiggerPockets Publishing LLC, Denver, CO
Copyright © 2021 by Scott Trench and Mindy Jensen
All Rights Reserved.

**Publisher's Cataloging-in-Publication data**
Names: Trench, Scott, author. | Jensen, Mindy, author.
Title: First-time home buyer : the complete playbook to avoiding rookie mistakes / by Scott Trench and Mindy Jensen.
Description: Includes bibliographical references. | Denver, CO: BiggerPockets Publishing, 2021.
Identifiers: LCCN: 2020941757 | ISBN 9780997584783 (pbk.) | 9780997584790 (ebook)
Subjects: LCSH House buying. | Real estate investment. | Personal finance. | BISAC BUSINESS & ECONOMICS / Real Estate / General | BUSINESS & ECONOMICS / Personal Finance / Investing | BUSINESS & ECONOMICS / Real Estate / Buying & Selling Homes
Classification: LCC HD1390.5 .T74 2021 | DDC 643/.12--dc23

**Printed on recycled paper in the United States of America**
10  9  8  7  6  5  4  3  2

# Dedication

## Scott

*For my wife, Virginia. I love you more than you know.*

*For my parents, Lynne and Randy, who have never wavered in their love and support for me.*

*For my friends (especially Walker and Annie), colleagues (especially Katie, Kaylee, and my co-author Mindy), and all the members of our community who have talked unendingly about REI and business with me and whose input helps me learn and grow every single day.*

## Mindy

*For Carl for all of his support. I can't imagine life without you.*

*For Claire and Daphne for being so patient with me while I was writing this.*

*For my parents, who showed me that moving into a new house is no big deal.*

*Huge thanks to Katie and Kaylee for letting us write this, and enormous thanks to Scott for being my writing partner.*

*Thanks to Morgan Housel for writing the article that sparked this whole idea.*

*And to Mrs. Satcher-Jones, sorry I was such a pain in tenth grade.*

# TABLE OF CONTENTS

# INTRODUCTION

It all starts with a simple concept: You want your dog to have a yard.

As you picture little Fido rolling around in green grass with ample space to roam, your thoughts wander further, and the simple concept turns into a dream. Maybe you don't want a roommate or to share walls with anyone else. Your upstairs neighbors stomp around like clumsy baby elephants. You want to paint the bedroom walls lime green and listen to Nickelback without fear of being overheard. Your landlord is, quite frankly, a bridge troll. You're throwing your money away on renting this place, anyway.

Suddenly, you're thinking of buying a house.

It's a no-brainer, right? Tax breaks! Long-term appreciation! Fixing up the outdated kitchen and adding hundreds of thousands of dollars in value! Just think of the possibilities!

Though the potential benefits are endless, we're here to give you some bad news—the potential problems are also endless. On the other end of the spectrum, you have broken toilets, wire fraud, and financial disaster that could spiral into endless debt and the possibility of foreclosure.

No pressure.

If you're reading this book, you are probably about to make what is the most significant financial decision of your life so far. Let's say that again: Buying a home is, first and foremost, a *financial decision*. Forget about your forbidden love of Nickelback, and forget all the people who have shouted from the rooftops that renting an apartment is worse than shoving all your cash down the garbage disposal (and then needing to call your landlord to fix your sink).

You've seen the workings of this financial decision before. Countless people buy their dream home right out of the gate—the huge, beautiful house on a hill, right in the middle of a winning school district and a charming neighborhood. They believe they are making a smart investment by finally breaking the renter's cycle. They throw their entire life savings at the painfully large down payment, but it doesn't stop there. The monthly mortgage payment sucks away a significant portion of each paycheck. With no cash left and an inability to save any more, they realize they walked right into a financial booby trap. They can't leave their job, start a business, move to Seattle, or travel the world like they always wanted.

Instead, they're stuck with their "smart investment" and all its broken toilets. That's the American dream, right?

Now, don't get us wrong. Buying a home really can be a smart investment that fast-tracks you to financial success, all while supporting a great quality of life. You can opt for a smaller home with a smaller mortgage and really rake in those tax benefits and long-term appreciation. You can even boogie your way into homeownership with the intention of turning your home into a *real* investment—that is, a rental property, a fix and flip, a basement Airbnb, or any other cash-generating asset. It's all about the things you know, the choices you make, and your willingness to see past the tempting house on a hill that exceeds your practical budget.

## THE STANDARD AMERICAN HOME PURCHASE

We're passionate about the power of real estate to build long-term wealth—but only if you make smart decisions when you purchase. What do those smart decisions look like?

Let's kick things off with a breakdown of the standard American home purchase, in all its ordinary glory.

Alex and Shelby have been hopping from apartment to apartment, and they're sick of the endless rules, security deposits, and pet rent. After getting married and settling into their newly wedded bliss, they decide it's time to buy a house—hooray for freedom!

Collectively, they make $85,000 per year and have $40,000 in lifetime savings outside of their retirement accounts. While shopping around for their first home, they move into a sublet apartment with a lease that ends in three months. They need to find a home before then to avoid signing a one-year extension.

To get started on their journey, they call a local lender to find out just how much house they can afford. Their lender tells them that their collective income and credit qualifies for a maximum mortgage loan of about $400,000. The monthly payment would be about $2,500, which is significantly higher than their current rent—but with the countless benefits of homeownership.

Here's a quick peek behind the scenes: Though Alex and Shelby are ecstatic that they qualify for a $400,000 home, their lender isn't totally unbiased. While the loan qualification is based on hard numbers, the lender's goal is to calculate the *largest* possible loan—because the larger the loan, the more money the lender makes in commission.

What does the happy couple do with this information? Well, they call up Joy, a local real estate agent whose face and phone number they saw on a bench ("These signs really work!"), and tell her they're shopping for their dream home with an all-in budget of $440,000—the $400,000 loan plus their $40,000 in cash.

Another look behind the scenes: Though Joy really wants her customers to be happy with their homes, she also earns a commission of 3 percent of each property's purchase price. The bigger the home, the bigger her commission. The faster she transacts, the more commissions she receives. Simply put, she helps local home buyers buy the most expensive homes possible in the shortest amount of time.

Joy asks the couple about their preferences—big yard, quiet street, newer build, close to amenities—and she takes them to neighborhoods where properties just so happen to be priced at $425,000 to $450,000 each. After a few showings, Joy presents them with a beautiful three-bedroom home that just came on the market in a darling neighborhood.

Alex and Shelby fall in love with the property. It's perfect. There are extra bedrooms for their future children, an unfinished basement that could be completed with a possible fourth bedroom, a huge garage, and a brand-new kitchen.

The problem? The home is listed at $485,000—just beyond their price range. But, hey, Alex and Shelby have fallen in love. This is their forever home, and they simply *have* to have it. Being the totally unbiased party that she is, Joy lets it slip that their lender will probably go for it if the couple can come up with a slightly larger down payment. Luckily, Alex's father is willing to lend them the remaining $40,000, as long as they pay him back gradually over time.

Because the property was just listed and is getting a lot of interest, Joy encourages the couple to submit a "competitive bid" at a few thousand dollars higher than the asking price. Alex and Shelby breathe a sigh of relief when their bid is accepted, and they go under contract on their dream home.

After a few tense weeks of negotiating with the seller, getting a home inspection, and signing endless contracts, Alex and Shelby close on their home. Their expert real estate agent, Joy, helped them navigate a few tricky situations, and she even negotiated $10,000 in concessions from the seller! Joy is a top agent, after all. (And she'll be making close to $15,000 on this transaction—talk about an incentive.)

The couple used the $40,000 they'd saved as a down payment, they have a $2,500 monthly mortgage payment, and they will pay back an additional $500 per month to Alex's dad for the next several years. They move into their dream home, and after settling in, they can't believe how responsible and mature they feel for finally moving forward on such a big milestone.

Life is bliss. (Or is it?)

## SO...WHAT'S THE PROBLEM?

Alex and Shelby's first-time home buyer situation seems par for the course. Little do they know, they're setting themselves up for a decades-long slog of financial struggle and worry. They've walked into an unseen financial booby trap that will consume the best part of their lives—that is, unless they win the lottery or receive a mysterious inheritance from Great Aunt Linda.

It took them five years to save up $40,000, build their credit, and get to $85,000 in joint income. Basically, all their cash savings and income (plus a little help from Dad) will now go toward the down payment and mortgage payments on their house. Their monthly expenses jump from $1,800 in rent to $2,500 toward their new mortgage (plus $500 per month to Alex's dad for the generous loan—which will take nearly seven years to pay back). On top of that, they assume all the *awesome* maintenance expenses that come with being a homeowner.

Alex and Shelby might have been saving money for years, but you can bet your bottom dollar they aren't saving much now. The mere concept of investing their money anywhere else (like in retirement accounts, stocks, or real estate) went right out the window when they closed on their house. The only "wealth" that Alex and Shelby have is the slowly building equity in their home.

As a result of this choice, Alex and Shelby are stuck. They can't change careers, and they can't change location. If an opportunity with a huge pay raise in another city comes up for Shelby, she can't take it—at least not in the near future. She has "invested" far too much in her new home to up and move. Because they are already taking the highest-paying jobs they can find in their local city, Alex and Shelby are unlikely to receive massive raises in the next few years.

Alex and Shelby are now "house poor." They spend everything they earn on their living expenses, massive monthly mortgage payment, and unexpected home maintenance costs. They must work their current high-paying jobs indefinitely, fighting to climb the corporate ladder. It'll take years, if not decades, of promotions and raises to finally return to a cash-flow-positive lifestyle, and only then do they have a shot at starting to save money again.

They're in a weak position if they want to start a business. They're in a tough spot if one parent wants to quit their job to raise their children. They can't do anything more than take a few low-cost vacations per year—they certainly can't take six months off and travel the world like they always dreamed of doing.

Alex and Shelby will slowly slip into the middle-class trap. They will passively accept the next phase of their careers to move up the corporate ladder one rung at a time. They will forget their dreams of being leaders in the community or spending significant time with their children during the formative years of their lives. They will basically live paycheck to paycheck, even if they build "home equity" on paper by paying down their mortgage and eventually benefiting from appreciation.

This struggle will continue for decades, but it will get better someday. Maybe ten or twenty years down the road, Alex and Shelby will reassess their financial position. They'll see a large increase in the value of their home, just like they knew would happen all those years ago. They're now sitting on several hundred thousand dollars of equity, driven by slowly paying down their mortgage and the long-term appreciation of their beautiful neighborhood.

They'll look back and talk about how their forever home was the best "investment" they ever made.

Well, of course it was! It was the *only* large investment they ever made.

By allowing the lure of the dream home to pull at their heartstrings (and their purse strings), they made a decision that will negatively impact their lives for decades. And guess what? It would be no surprise if they build those hundreds of thousands of dollars of equity just to sell their home to buy a bigger, better, nicer home down the street.

# WHY YOU SHOULD CARE

Alex and Shelby may have struggled for a while, but it all worked out in the end. And besides, your great-great-grandpa bought his house when it was only $300, and now it's worth $300,000—so why not follow in his footsteps?

Well, the times they are a-changing, and the American dream just won't cut it anymore.

Not only is the current financial situation wildly different than in great-great-grandpa's day—high rental costs make it difficult to save for a down payment, and an increase in education debt makes it difficult to apply for a mortgage[1]—but the concept of retirement isn't what it used to be. Younger generations have recognized the change and are rolling with the punches: They're cutting frivolous spending and handling their future retirement with a much more self-sufficient approach. The concept of "financial freedom" allows folks to retire early, evade the corporate rat race, and follow their dreams.

The same changes apply to homes and mortgages: Millennials are, on average, delaying getting married, having fewer children, and buying smaller houses.[2] Why try to keep up with an outdated standard? Buying a home that stretches your financial limits is a socially accepted practice that has gone unchallenged for far too long, but that's starting to change.

It's time for a new kind of homeownership, one that does a lot more than just put a roof over your head. A smart home-buying decision will not only give you a place to live but also offer flexibility, financial stability,

---

**1** Jung Choi, Bhargavi Ganesh, Laurie Goodman, Sarah Strochak, and Jun Zhu, "Millennial Homeownership: Why Is It So Low, and How Can We Increase It?" Housing Finance Policy Center, July 2018, accessed at https://www.urban.org/sites/default/files/publication/98729/millennial_homeownership_0.pdf.

**2** Sheri Koones, "Why Millennials Are Buying Smaller, More Efficient Houses," Forbes, October 18, 2019, https://www.forbes.com/sites/sherikoones/2019/10/18/why-millennials-are-buying-smaller-more-efficient-houses/#7e8887524558.

and the chance to recognize an increase in that home's value over time. By following all the steps outlined in this book, you will set yourself up for a smart home purchase at a great price, with as few snags as possible in the process.

# STRANGER DANGER

Since you're about to make a whopper of a financial choice and you're going to follow our advice while doing it, allow us to introduce ourselves (and toot our own horns).

We're both experts on finance, home buying, and real estate investing, and we have more than thirty years of experience between us. We're cohosts of *The BiggerPockets Money Podcast*, which has been around since 2018 and (as of now) has more than 10 million downloads, 1,500 five-star reviews, and countless corny dad jokes. The show covers everything you can and should do to get your finances in order so you can save, invest, and ultimately win at life. After hundreds of interviews with brilliant financial experts, we have absorbed quite a bit of knowledge.

On the home-buying side, Mindy knows best. She's been buying and selling homes as an investor for more than twenty years, and she's been a licensed real estate agent for more than six. Mindy is currently occupying her eleventh live-in flip—which means she buys wonderfully hideous houses, moves in, makes them beautiful while living there, and sells them for a killer profit.

On the finance side, Scott knows his stuff—he's the CEO of BiggerPockets.com and author of the best-selling finance book *Set for Life*. Not to mention that he achieved financial freedom and built a successful real estate business just three years after graduating college. (Yes, seriously.)

All horn tooting aside, we're here to help you make the best decision possible when it comes to buying your first home. We've seen both ends of the spectrum—the crash-and-burns and the wild success stories—and are happy to pass this knowledge along to you. Buying your first house can be intimidating, and it can sometimes seem like no one will give you a straight answer to all your questions.

Well, buckle up, buttercup: straight answers ahead.

# WHAT YOU'LL FIND IN THIS BOOK

Dad jokes and puns? Most likely.

But other than that, this book encourages new (and improved) frameworks about the home-buying process. If you're looking to justify your dream home as an "investment," you'll find no help here.

The first part of this book will cover the critical financial concepts behind buying a house, plus the different strategies you can use to upgrade your first home to a real, cash-positive investment. Before diving into a home purchase, you should fully understand what's at stake so you can make a focused decision. Part One will educate you on the financial benefits (and consequences) of a home purchase and demonstrate a range of possible home purchase decisions.

Buh-bye, American dream—hello, financial freedom!

The second part of this book is all about preparation. Now that you know you're *ready* to buy a house, it's time to make some real-life decisions. We'll show you how to figure out exactly what you want from a home, define what a "good" deal really means to you, and organize your finances. We'll also touch on how to understand your loan, choose a stellar lender, and find a real estate agent with your best interests in mind.

Getting that first set of house keys is a milestone, a rite of passage, a feel-good moment. But getting to that point, not so much. The home-buying process is like digging through an unorganized box of holiday decorations—it's full of chaos and unpleasant surprises, and no one in the world seems to know what you'll encounter. (What's title insurance, you ask? You're about to find out.) That's why Part Three will focus on the nitty-gritty process behind home buying.

By the end of it all, not only will you see homeownership in a new light, but you'll be armed with the tips, tricks, and tactics you need to really go for it. And, done correctly, your first home purchase should give you better odds of fulfilling your dreams, achieving your potential, and building a strong financial foundation. Fido gets a yard, you get to travel the world, everyone is happy.

You might even get to have uncomfortable conversations with your friends and family who just don't get it. Why not buy the house on a hill if you can afford it (at least on paper)? Why subject yourself to hard work and hustle when you've spent all this time saving money for a down payment already? You're going to do *what* with your detached garage?

We're not sorry. Let's dive in!

# FIRST-TIME HOME BUYER ROADMAP

STRATEGIZE　　PREPARE　　CHOOSE A LENDER & GET PREAPPROVED　　FIND & HIRE A GREAT AGENT　　SEARCHING FOR & VIEWING PROPERTIES　　MAKING OFFERS

**LOAN UNDERWRITING**

| UNDER CONTRACT | HOME INSPECTION | DUE DILIGENCE | APPRAISAL | CLOSING TIME | HOMEOWNER |

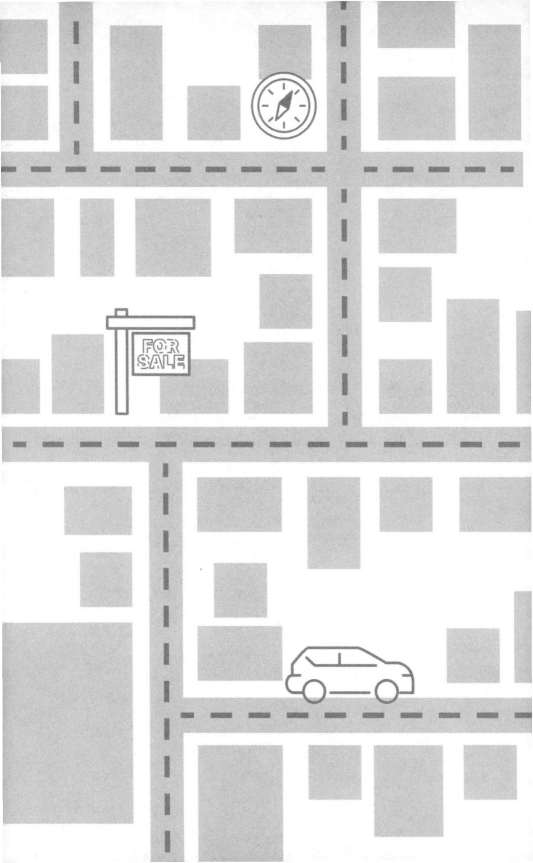

# PART ONE

# HOME-BUYING STRATEGY

*"You do not find the happy life. You make it."*

—CAMILLA EYRING KIMBALL

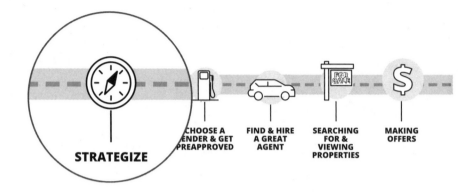

STRATEGIZE | CHOOSE A LENDER & GET PREAPPROVED | FIND & HIRE A GREAT AGENT | SEARCHING FOR & VIEWING PROPERTIES | MAKING OFFERS

CHAPTER ONE

# IS BUYING A HOUSE A GOOD INVESTMENT?

So, is it?

Answer the question. Don't hold back. Say your answer out loud, especially if you're in a public place.

Chances are your gut reaction stems from years of social conditioning—and that answer is *yes*. Most of the adults you know own a house. Some might be an utterly practical three-bed two-bath, while some others are a second vacation home on a lake in rural Vermont. Houses are cozy, private, wonderful little structures that give us shelter.

Is there anything wrong with buying a house? Of course not. But is it a good *investment*?

The easiest way to demonstrate the lack of clarity here is to take a look at the financial impact of buying versus renting over the long term. For the sake of this example and to keep things simple, we'll assume some specific numbers, but these are subject to change depending on where you live and when you're reading this. The main point, however, applies across many of the major markets in the country.

# RENTING VERSUS BUYING

*In the left corner, weighing in at $2,300 per month...*

Renting a lovely apartment! The original listing included words like "sun-soaked" and "pet-friendly," and you have everything you need, give or take a few overdue maintenance requests.

Your $2,300 rent includes all expenses, utilities, and routine fixes. Over the course of a year, that monthly payment adds up to a total of $27,600. (Yeah, just let that number sink in for a minute.) You can also assume your rent will increase annually in line with inflation at an average of 3.4 percent per year. Next year, that $2,300 per month becomes $2,378 per month, then $2,459 the year after that.

Of course, you won't build any equity in the property you live in, but you only have to pay that simple $2,300 per month to enjoy your sun-soaked paradise.

*And in the right corner, current world heavyweight champion...*

Buying a house! Though buying a home means owning a slice of property, homeownership is not nearly as straightforward as sending off a monthly rent payment.

Let's start with the hard numbers. This house is listed at $400,000. The buyer makes a 10 percent down payment and pays 3 percent of the property's value in closing costs: an all-in total of $52,000 cash to close on the property. The buyer then assumes a loan of $360,000 (the purchase price minus the down payment), and with all interest, taxes, and insurance included, the buyer's monthly mortgage payment is $2,917 per month. Because broken windows and running water aren't free, let's tack on an extra $250 per month for maintenance and utilities. This comes to a total cost of $3,167 per month, or $38,000 per year.

Simple enough, right? The home buyer obviously pays more per year than the renter.

That's true, but it's not so easy. We also need to take into consideration all those wonderful benefits of homeownership. The first and most obvious would be building equity—part of that $2,917 monthly payment will pay off the total loan balance. The property will also appreciate (that is, increase in value) at an average rate of 3.4 percent per year. Appreciation is complicated, but for the sake of this example, let's say the $400,000 home will be worth $413,600 this time next year, then $427,662 the year after that.

Though this sounds wonderful, you can't forget that this daring home buyer brought $52,000 in hard cash to close on the house. (And by *hard cash,* we don't mean stowed in a sketchy briefcase—we mean real money, not credit, from a bank account.) Because the buyer's mortgage payments come out to $38,000 per year, that means the buyer spends a total of $90,000 just in the first year.

That $27,600 per year to live in an apartment is starting to sound really good, isn't it?

To clarify, the two main comparisons we're looking at are:

- **Up-front cost.** In this example, the apartment renter has no up-front cost, while the home buyer has $52,000. Both will vary based on the specific situation—sometimes, you have to put down a deposit before renting an apartment, and sometimes you can buy a home with a lower down payment—but no matter what, you're bound to pay more up front to own a home.
- **Total net worth created or destroyed.** Your net worth is the whole kit and caboodle of your financial health. Squander all your savings on a porcelain doll collection? That's a loss in your net worth. Invent America's first pizza vending machine? Cha-ching. Spend all your savings on a down payment but then slowly build equity in a property? That's a big initial hit that eventually regains value over time.

Let's look at a visual of our two competitors in both these categories.

## Cash Outlays: Next 10 Years

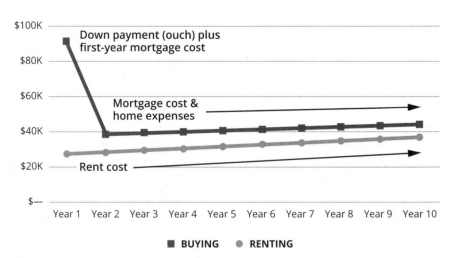

Starting with that up-front cost, you can see how financially painful that first year of owning a home can really be. Even by year ten, the homeowner is still paying more each year than the renter. (Remember, the cost of rent is increasing by 3.4% every year, while the cost of the monthly mortgage payment is locked in place.) You can imagine that around year fifteen, the homeowner will be paying less each year—but who really has a robust fifteen-year plan?

But in the meantime, here's the important thing: The homeowner is going to be shelling out more cash over the next ten years. They'll have less disposable income for fun things like road trips and karaoke bar nights, and it'll be harder for them to invest in stocks, real estate, or retirement accounts.

Now, this is where the fun begins:

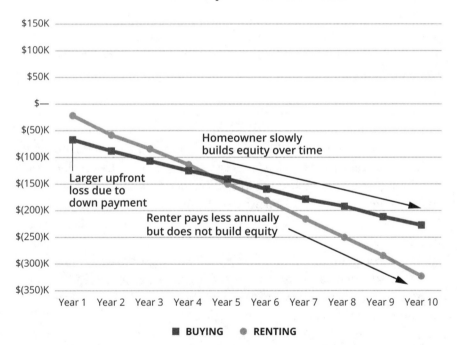

## Net Worth Impact: Next 10 Years

Homeowner slowly builds equity over time

Larger upfront loss due to down payment

Renter pays less annually but does not build equity

■ BUYING   ● RENTING

Right out of the gate, our homeowner line is looking a little droopy. That large up-front down payment plus closing costs takes a toll on the homeowner's net worth, but around year five, things start to change.

Because the homeowner has been paying down their mortgage (and not tossing their money at a landlord "make it rain" style), they're building equity in their home. That, combined with the gradually increasing value of their property, starts to counteract the costs, and by year five, their net worth is less impacted by housing than the renter's.

Is it better to buy or rent in this scenario? All other financial factors like cash savings and credit score aside, buying might be better for someone who plans to stay in the property for longer than five years or so. The break-even point can vary considerably depending on the numbers; you can conduct your own analysis with the rent-versus-buy spreadsheet at www.biggerpockets.com/homebuyerbonus.

Still, if the buyer decides to hit the road in year two, they can't simply sell the house and get back all the money they put into it. Let's say this buyer's plans change, and they need to relocate for a new job after two years of owning their home. The $400,000 home is worth about $425,000 after two years of average appreciation, and we can assume that the loan balance would be about $349,000 after the down payment and regular monthly mortgage payments. The $25,000 gain in property value, $40,000 down payment, and $11,000 in loan paydown seems like a lot of money that they will "get back" when they sell, but that's not necessarily the case.

Including the initial $12,000 they paid in closing costs when they bought the house plus an overall mortgage cost of $38,000 per year, they will have spent a total of $88,000 in two years—and that doesn't even account for the cost of any property maintenance. Also, if they want someone to take the house off their hands, they'll have to pay seller's closing costs, usually around 7.5 percent of the home's value, just to close that transaction. If they sell the property at $425,000, that's another $32,000 out of pocket.

While they built a total of $76,000 in home equity—a combination of the $40,000 down payment, $25,000 of appreciation, and $11,000 of loan paydown—they spent a total of $120,000 over the course of their two-year housing venture. Ouch.

Long story short, buying a house costs money—a *lot* of it—but will help you build equity and wealth over long time periods relative to renting. The transaction costs associated with buying and selling property often make renting a better choice if you don't intend to own long term. The math skews even more in favor of renting instead of buying in high-cost-of-living areas like New York City or San Francisco because of these high transaction costs and high property values.

Scott conducted this analysis, with these numbers, in July 2020— and contrary to what you might expect from a real estate investor, his decision was to be a *renter* with his personal residence. Given his desired lifestyle plus his wants and needs for housing, renting was the better option. Scott plans to live in the location for no more than three or four years, and he will, of course, invest the cash not required for mortgage payments or down payments in other real estate investments.

# OPPORTUNITY COST

Remember when we talked about the homeowner not being able to enjoy as many road trips and karaoke bar nights? Though they'll miss belting out "Wonderwall" with their buddies, they'll also miss out on something much bigger—the opportunity to invest that money elsewhere. This concept is called *opportunity cost*.

The word "investment" carries a heavy burden, especially in the context of buying a home. In many cases, a primary residence produces investment returns far below what can be expected from other assets.

Picture this: The renter saves up the same $52,000 that the home buyer does, but instead of moving into a house, they keep renting and use those savings to invest in stocks. With an average stock market return of 10 percent each year, they're actually building *more* equity than the homeowner, at least in the beginning. Adding this to our equation actually pushes that break-even point for renting versus buying to about year six.

In most scenarios, a rent-versus-buy analysis will reveal a break-even point between year four and year six. If you're right on the cusp of the five-year mark, you might be tempted to just go ahead and buy instead of rent. So many people have benefitted from insane appreciation, right? They wake up one day and their home is worth twice as much as what they bought it for.

Don't give in to the temptation. If you're not sure how long you'll stay in a home, we recommend that you err on the side of renting, not buying. If you have an investor mindset, you have a strong chance of realizing opportunities elsewhere—like with stocks or true real estate investing— in addition to building even larger cash savings. Betting on appreciation is not a great way to get your money back.

# LESS IS MORE

We still haven't answered that initial question: *Is buying a home a good investment?* The $35 trillion housing market is overwhelmed with the same language: *This home is a great investment, a good starter home that has huge potential, it's such a steal!* This message is reinforced in countless ways culturally and socially. As a result, millions of people have more wealth in their home equity than in all other "investments" combined.

Though the rent-versus-buy case study is an effective way to demonstrate the pros and cons of buying a house, it's not the be-all and end-all. It's tempting to look at these graphs and conclude that because buying a home destroys less wealth than renting over a long period of time, buying is the better long-term investment.

To that, we say: Look at the graphs again. What do you notice about the left-side axis of that net worth graph?

All. Those. Numbers. Are. Negative.

Buying a home does not create wealth (except in a few extreme cases, which we'll touch on later). In fact, buying a home destroys wealth. Any type of housing destroys wealth. Whether it's a rent check to your landlord or a mortgage payment to your lender, that's money out of your pocket and into the pocket of someone else.

Is buying a home a good investment? Trick question. Buying a home is not an investment. It's one cost among many in your life—it's the cost to put a roof over your head. Are your groceries a good investment? They may be saving you more money than buying all-you-can-eat sushi every night, but your pot of homemade chili is not putting money in your pocket. Unfortunately.

If you still don't believe us, let's put it this way: At best, buying a home under the impression that it's an investment could leave you in a slightly better financial position versus renting over the long term. However, at worst, it could result in hundreds of thousands of wasted dollars, and even more than that in opportunity cost. Basically, the less money you spend on housing—whether that's rent or mortgage—the less wealth you destroy. The more affordable your lifestyle, the more options you have, and the better off you'll be financially.

Instead of buying a massive dream home under the impression that it's an investment, you could use your savings to start a chili food truck business with your secret recipe and make millions.

Chilions?

Sorry, we couldn't resist.

# CHAPTER SUMMARY

- The longer you plan to stay in a house, the more likely your choice to buy rather than rent will prove a good one. The goal is for a combination of loan paydown and increase in property value over time to offset the high transactional costs of buying and selling a house.
- The more potential for appreciation your property has, the better off you'll be buying relative to renting. Appreciation is a tricky thing to plan around, but there's no denying it's a powerful force. There are some tricks you can use to force appreciation's hand, which we'll cover in Chapter Three.
- Say it again for the people in the back: Buying a house is not an investment. It's not always a bad choice, but it's not an *investment*.
- We made our first food pun. Didn't we tell you there would be some terrible jokes in here?

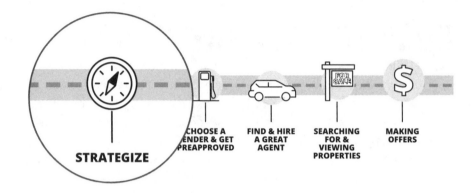

STRATEGIZE
CHOOSE A LENDER & GET PREAPPROVED
FIND & HIRE A GREAT AGENT
SEARCHING FOR & VIEWING PROPERTIES
MAKING OFFERS

CHAPTER TWO

# UNDERSTANDING EXIT OPTIONS

For all our talk about buying a house for the long term, you're probably going to have to leave your first home eventually. With all the excitement of buying, many people forget to plan for the inevitable move-out—but the truth is, an average homeowner moves five to seven years after their first purchase.

Chances are, you're *not* getting a "forever home" the first time around. You'll make sacrifices when you choose a home in your price range, and those sacrifices will start to haunt your nightmares. Maybe you'll just outgrow your small home—or maybe you'll get so sick of looking at popcorn ceilings that you'll never touch a bag of popcorn again. Even if your first home is absolutely perfect, you are likely to move for business or personal reasons at some point down the line.

What's the best way to deal with the dreaded eventual move-out? While we'd love to give you tips on packing boxes and going through storage junk, we mean financially—what's the best way to move out and sell your home without losing a whole moving-truck load of money?

There are many different strategies for leaving a house behind, and those strategies are called *exit options*. One way to save your future self a thousand headaches is to think about your exit options *before* you buy your house. (It's like making an appearance at a party when you don't want to stick around for awkward conversation—you have to formulate an exit plan prior to showing up.) If you wait until a new job or personal emergency forces you to relocate, the external pressure will make for a lousy decision.

Do yourself a favor and don't assume that your first, exciting home purchase will be your last. Before you get caught up in the whirlwind of the buying process, take your exit into consideration. A well-prepared buyer will find a home with one or more of the following exit options, though a savvy buyer will maximize their potential across all three options for the most flexibility and the best chance for building wealth.

1. **Live in the property indefinitely.** Meaning, you have to actually enjoy living there. If popcorn ceilings give you the heebie-jeebies, keep that in mind when you're shopping for a home.
2. **Keep the property as a cash-flowing rental.** Meaning, the property must generate cash flow as a rental. Don't panic—we'll get to the details later.
3. **Sell the property for a net profit.** Meaning, the property must appreciate enough to offset all those pesky closing costs we talked about in the previous chapter.

Controlling the variables that impact the financial outcome of a home purchase isn't easy. Long-term appreciation rates, property taxes, home insurance rates, and local rent prices are anyone's guess at the end of the day. While you can lean a little on national and local averages, you certainly can't depend on them.

However, there's one variable completely within the buyer's control that can dramatically change the risk associated with a home purchase: the amount of time you own the property. We've said it before and we'll say it again, but this time there's a bonus—buying a home is a long-term choice, but you don't necessarily have to *live* in the property long term to *own* it long term.

With that, let's dive a little deeper into each of your three exit options.

# EXIT STRATEGY NO. 1
# LIVE IN THE PROPERTY INDEFINITELY

A big problem for many first-timers is buying too much house too early in life, which limits their financial options. Do you remember our good friends Alex and Shelby from the introduction? Not only did they buy at the very top of their budget, but they also borrowed extra money from Dad on top of that.

While buying such a big house was destructive to their financial health, the polar opposite wouldn't have been helpful either. If Alex and Shelby had decided to save hundreds of thousands of dollars by purchasing a dilapidated shack in the middle of a cornfield, they wouldn't exactly be living their best lives.

Although purchasing a McMansion outside of your price range is a problem, getting so hung up on the numbers that you buy a house you absolutely hate is equally silly. We know that the average homeowner lives in their first property for five to seven years, and generally speaking, the younger they are, the less time they will live in their current home. Therefore, you should buy a house that you can enjoy—or, at the very least, tolerate—for five to seven years.

This is the exit option on which we'll spend the least amount of time, since hardly anyone will buy a house that doesn't meet their lifestyle expectations. However, we'll sometimes come across folks who are so overeager to max out their savings potential that they end up in a (metaphorical) cornfield.

Everyone has different priorities when it comes to houses. Whether yours include the year it was built, the school district, proximity to your workplace, square footage, kitchen updates, or the space and potential to start your own backyard beekeeping hobby, you must understand what is a "want" and what is a "need."

If you, your partner, or your family are unhappy with the location, build, size, lack of beekeeping space, or other unchangeable aspects of your house, you're not reaping one of the best benefits of home buying: the freedom to prioritize the things that are most important to you! You're also putting your money at risk, since you'll feel increasing pressure to move out, and you might make decisions that are against your long-term interests.

Not everything has to be perfect, but you should keep your needs in mind. Just make sure to...bee smart about such a long-term choice.

# EXIT STRATEGY NO. 2: KEEP THE PROPERTY AS A CASH-FLOWING RENTAL

Like we said before, don't panic. We'll go into much more detail about how to analyze your home as a rental, look for income potential, and think about the various aspects of cash flow in Chapter Four. For now, the important thing to know is that, as a homeowner, you should have a reasonable understanding of your property's performance if you were to move out and rent it out to others.

Whether or not you want to be someone else's landlord, you should at least consider the option when purchasing your home. If the property is primed to make more income than it costs, you're putting yourself in a great position to create wealth down the road.

Many people plan for the rental option but don't analyze the numbers properly. A home that "bleeds" (a morbid word for bringing rent that's less than the cost of maintenance) can be a huge drag on your finances and flexibility. You don't want to pay for a bleeding property that you're not even living in, so we'll pay close attention to these numbers in Chapter Four.

If the walls of your property are actually bleeding, the house is probably haunted. You should get that checked out.

# EXIT STRATEGY NO. 3: SELL THE PROPERTY FOR A NET PROFIT

Because home prices tend to increase in line with inflation, a majority of buyers automatically expect their purchase to appreciate over the long term.

I'm sure you expect us to cause a fuss about this, but we don't actually think it's an issue. If you randomly select a home anywhere in the United States, buy it, and hold it for thirty years, then yes—over time, that home's value is likely to experience a 3.4 percent average annual increase. Certain markets across the country will wax and wane, but there's no reason to dispute the average historical rates.

The problem with relying on appreciation is the fact that it's not a smooth, continuous progression. Though we like to use 3.4 percent in a lot of our equations and estimates (like the $400,000 home that was worth $425,000 after two years), it's not actually that simple.

Appreciation rates can be volatile, especially when looking at a smaller range of time. This was made clearly and painfully evident by the 2008 housing market crash. Many who purchased homes in 2007 saw years go by in which their property was worth less than they paid for it. However, if they keep holding on to those properties for a long period of time, they are more likely to see a rebound from that painful drop in value.

The median home price in 2007 (adjusted for inflation) was about $270,000. The number continued to drop into 2012, when it reached a low of $193,000—which looks like an irreparable $77,000 loss. However, a slow increase into 2019 saw the median home price rise back to $270,000.[3] Though twelve years is a long time to wait for a home to return to its original value, the 2008 market crash is obviously a special case—and a perfect example of why you can't depend on appreciation in the short term.

When houses are selling like pumpkin spice in November, it's considered a seller's market, since sellers benefit the most. When houses are slow to sell, it's considered a buyer's market, since buyers will benefit the most from more housing inventory and less competition. Both markets come and go over the years. If you purchase a property and hope that a seller's market will come around (or stay around) and profit will fall into your lap, you are completely at the mercy of the unpredictable market. Whether or not you're able to sell your home (and when) will be out of your control.

Luckily, market appreciation is not the only way that your home might increase in value. Instead of letting an uncertain market control your choices, you can instead give yourself the highest probability of selling your home quickly and for a profit. In the next chapter, we'll show you how to make reasonable assumptions about the long-term appreciation rate you can expect from your home purchase. We'll also dive into some of the practical, accessible ways you can *force* appreciation—which is an assertive-sounding way to say that you can add value to your home on your own. The higher the odds you have of market appreciation and the more ways you can force short-term appreciation, the better.

# CHAPTER SUMMARY

- Think about your exit options before you buy a house. There are three main ways your future self can deal with a property: just

---

3  PK, "Historical Home Prices: Monthly Median Value in the US from 1953–2020," DQYDJ, September 5, 2020, https://dqydj.com/historical-home-prices/.

keep living in it, turn it into a rental, or sell it for a profit. The more exit options you have, the better. If you're able to find a house that is pleasant to live in, holds its own as a future rental, and has a high chance of short-term appreciation, you've basically won the homeowner lottery.

- Appreciation is a scary variable (scariable?), especially in the short term. The national average works when looking twenty or thirty years into the future, but massive fluctuations can happen between now and then. If you want to be able to count on selling your home for a profit in five or so years, it's best to take a different approach.

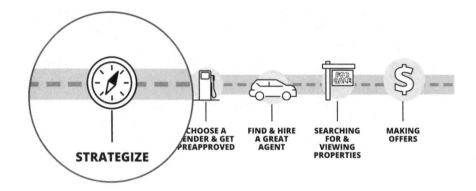

STRATEGIZE · CHOOSE A LENDER & GET PREAPPROVED · FIND & HIRE A GREAT AGENT · SEARCHING FOR & VIEWING PROPERTIES · MAKING OFFERS

CHAPTER THREE

# HOW TO TAKE CONTROL OF APPRECIATION

Although we've talked plenty about appreciation up to this point, let's start this chapter with a basic definition, in case you've started skipping around. (Do what you will, but you might have missed some top-shelf puns—and we all know that's what you're really here for.)

Simply put, appreciation is the increase in a property's value over time. If you bought a house for $200,000 and it's worth $300,000 the next year, it has appreciated. By a lot. You should be appreciative of that appreciation.

"Appreciation" itself is a very general term, but there are two more specific subtypes: *market appreciation* and *forced appreciation*. The former is what we've been mentioning extensively—the national, regional, and local factors that give your home's value a little more oomph each year. The latter is a fancy way to talk about adding value to the home itself, like fixing up a relic of the 1970s by removing the shag carpet and wood paneling. These may sound like two completely different concepts, but they're both just different ways a house can increase in value over time.

Much like exit options, you should be thinking about appreciation *before* you buy your house instead of as a panicked afterthought. In this chapter, not only will we discuss a framework for thinking about these value-adds, but we'll talk about the best ways to incorporate them into your home-buying strategy.

# MARKET APPRECIATION

Because we need a starting point to discuss market appreciation, let's take a minute to talk about national averages. There are many different ways to look at appreciation, but we personally prefer something called the Case-Shiller Index.[4] Without going too deep into the details, this index basically tracks the sales prices of single-family properties sold at market value, which excludes apartments, condos, co-ops, new construction, foreclosures, and selling a house to a friend for a favorable price.

Why is it important to ignore new home construction? New builds tend to get bigger and bigger in square footage, with better floor plans, gizmos, and gadgets. The average purchase price of new homes increases at a rate of nearly 5 percent per year on average, so they give us a completely different picture on price movements. Because we want to estimate how much a home purchased today will be worth in the future, we should look at the more accurate appreciation rate of existing homes, not new ones.

The Case-Shiller Index is where we got the number we have mentioned in previous chapters—that 3.4 percent appreciation rate we hold near and dear to our hearts. This national average encompasses existing houses nationwide, and though it's unpredictable on a year-to-year basis, it's statistically consistent over the long term.

However, if you want a more dependable way to gauge appreciation over the next decade or less, it's better to zoom in on a more specific location.

## Regional Appreciation

Though the country as a whole follows a consistent long-term pattern, different regions around the country experience different levels of appreciation. Their short-term changes and long-term averages can

---

4  Amy Fontinelle, "Understanding the Case-Shiller Housing Index," Investopedia, February 11, 2020, https://www.investopedia.com/articles/mortgages-real-estate/10/understanding-case-shiller-index.asp.

vary considerably from the national average. (You can't expect us all to have the exact same housing market when we can't even agree on how to pronounce "pecan.")

In addition to the Case-Shiller national index, there are many market-specific indexes that can be helpful when buying your first home. For example, the Composite 20 is a home price index for twenty major metropolitan statistical areas, including Los Angeles, New York, Dallas, and Seattle, among others.

Localized tools use methods similar to Case-Shiller's to estimate appreciation in specific areas. For example, Denver home prices have experienced a 4.2 percent annualized appreciation rate from 2000 to 2020. Detroit, on the other hand, has experienced an appreciation rate much closer to zero over the same period. In both cases, the local average is more useful than the national figure for estimating a home's future appreciation.

On the other hand, you might look at your market and think that historical averages are no longer useful for predicting the future. If you live in San Francisco—an area that has seen massive appreciation in recent years—you might speculate that high housing prices combined with increasing opportunities for remote work will motivate professionals to leave in favor of more affordable cities. Maybe you live in an area that hasn't appreciated much in the past, but a local organic bakery was featured on Food Network, and your town has been "discovered." In either case, appreciation rates could deviate significantly from their previous averages.

In addition, past performance is not a guarantee of future success. A Denver investor might also assume that appreciation will slow down over the next twenty years because they feel that prices simply can't climb much higher than they are today. The Detroit investor might think that Detroit is about to hit a growth spurt and prices will increase over the next few decades.

The best you can do is try to understand the basics of your market and make an assumption you can live with. Is your city a growing metropolis with lifestyle opportunities and jobs that are likely to attract more high-earning professionals over time? Or is your area on the decline, with more people leaving than moving in every year? Ask yourself about the specifics of this location in the context of the recent past and foreseeable future, and you'll be in a better position to ballpark long-term appreciation at, above, or below the national average of 3.4 percent.

Why is the exactness of this number important, you ask? Two, 3, 4 percent—it's all adding some sort of value, right? The truth is, a few percentage points can throw off the numbers considerably. For example, that $400,000 home in our previous example would be worth $473,000 after five years at the 3.4 percent national average appreciation rate. What if that house had been in Nashville, which has seen a massive 6 percent average annual increase in value? In that same period of time with an ongoing rate of growth, that house would be worth $535,000—which is a huge overall difference for just a few percentage points.

Exciting equity aside, this rate is one of the key factors behind your decision to buy or rent—it changes that critical break-even point considerably. A home that appreciates at a 6 percent rate would be a better option than renting, even if you stay in the home for only three years before selling. The higher appreciation rate makes it easier to "earn back" the money that is put into buying and selling a home.

However, always keep in mind that appreciation rates ultimately provide nothing more than a gut check. Should you base your entire home-buying decision on what you think the market might do after five years? Probably not. There's no way to reliably forecast appreciation rates in the short or long term—at least, not until someone invents a time machine. We're patiently waiting for that day.

While we acknowledge the fact that it is one big, whopping guess, we also need to acknowledge that some markets are more likely to experience growth than others. It's important to at least form a hypothesis about future appreciation rates in your local market as you go into your home-buying decision. If you are buying in a market in which you expect appreciation at a faster rate than the national average, you need to be sure those expectations are justified. Similarly, if you're buying in a market that experiences less growth, you should factor those expectations into your assessment.

## Hyper-Local Factors

It's a beautiful day in the neighborhood. The sun is shining, birds are chirping, and...the sketchy gas station next door is getting robbed by an escaped convict from the prison down the street.

When it comes to the hyper-local features that can impact your property's value (and your own quality of life), an infinite number of factors can come into play. The bad news is that we can't possibly address them all. The good news is that you can probably see and hear most of them with your own eyes and ears.

Start by driving around the block surrounding any home that you are considering buying. How busy are the streets? How well kept are the houses and their yards? Pay particularly close attention to any busy streets and commercial buildings near your property, especially if it's in a city or suburb. A lovely grocery store a few blocks away? That's a plus. Easy access to a highway or airport? Double plus. Being so close to the airport that planes are constantly zooming over your roof? Not so much.

Look for anything that makes you feel uncomfortable or is just objectively unsightly or seedy. There's no excuse for buying a house, living there for a week, then being caught by surprise by the "gentleman's club" you didn't realize was three blocks down the road.

Ask yourself how these neighborhood features will impact your own standard of living, then consider how they will impact the life of a hypothetical, picky future home buyer to whom you're trying to sell the home. Imagine them walking around your house, gushing about the hardwood floors and spacious yard, then stepping outside to a breath of fresh air that smells peculiarly like the dog food factory across the street.

Though you may be able to fix up the ugly features of a home itself, you need to keep in mind all those neighborhood features you can't possibly alter. Petition all you want, but you won't be able to shut down that dog food factory, and the delicious aroma of dog food can significantly slow your home's appreciation rate over time.

Once you're done scouting the location as it is now, ask yourself what the neighborhood will look like at different times of the year. For example, in a snowy part of the country, a home with a driveway facing south will see snow melt faster than a home facing north. Is the direction the house faces a deal breaker? No. Is it something to file away when deciding between two otherwise similar properties? Absolutely.

Also be aware of activities that vary by season. A home next to a football stadium will bring fun lifestyle opportunities on game days, but it will also bring traffic jams, congestion, and maybe a bit of litter. A home next to a school offers a great opportunity for families to send their kiddos over without a commute, but it also brings daily bus and foot traffic during the school year. You might not be able to see these things if you purchase your home on a sleepy summer day, so try to ask local residents how the atmosphere varies in the area throughout the year.

Also note that seasonal patterns can be a good thing—some people will pay more, not less, to own a house that's close to exciting events in their community. The main point is to limit surprises down the road. Go into the purchase with your eyes (and ears and nostrils) wide open.

## Be the Worst That You Can Be

While you conduct your neighborhood analysis, circling the block like a very persistent (or very lost) salesperson, ask yourself whether the house you want to buy is the best on the block, the worst, or somewhere in between.

Buying the best home on the block might earn you bragging rights but will leave you with fewer potential buyers down the line. The nicest house will be dragged down by the properties in worse condition nearby, so its long-term appreciation rate is likely to be stifled.

On the other hand, the worst home on the block will have an appreciation rate that is bolstered by its fancier and better-maintained neighbors. Future buyers who might not otherwise consider your neighborhood because it's normally out of their price range could be interested in your property when you go to sell. There's also a lot more potential to force appreciation, but even if you don't want to take on the responsibility of a fixer-upper, a "in-between" house is still better than the best one.

Though you should be able to rank a neighborhood's homes by driving around, you can also support your best/worst/in-between conclusion based on the price of those houses. If you're buying a home for $350,000 in a neighborhood where they usually sell for $400,000, you're on the right track. If a home's price is $500,000 in that same neighborhood, not so much. Where could that $500,000 house possibly go from there? Plus, who would want to buy it down the line, when they could instead look at nicer neighborhoods that are full of half-million-dollar houses?

Just make sure you're not limiting your pool of potential buyers when you do decide to sell. Buying the worst house on the block can be a great approach, and you might even bring the property up to par with your fancy neighbors over time.

## Wrapping Up Market Appreciation

When considering appreciation rates, the best anyone can do is make an informed decision based on the concepts above. It is nearly impossible for the average home buyer to predict prices in the short term, but it is reasonable to make high-level assumptions over the long term. Start with the national long-term appreciation rate, adjust that based on your local market, and adjust again for the specifics of the location you choose within that market.

A home in a fast-growing city, next to a popular park and high-end grocery stores, in a great school district, that is also the worst home on its block is likely to experience a wonderful appreciation rate. It's much better off than the nicest home on the block, in a stagnating market, near seedy commercial retail, with a school district that would make Ferris Bueller cry. In one case, the buyer might reasonably assume a 4 to 5 percent long-term annual appreciation rate. In the other, they might assume a more modest 1 to 2 percent appreciation rate.

The buyer shouldn't rely on appreciation in either case, since the economy could tank tomorrow and leave them with reduced property values. They should position themselves to potentially recognize appreciation by buying the right property, but the appreciation itself is just icing on the cake.

# FORCED APPRECIATION

Though market ups and downs typically come to mind when you hear the word "appreciation", there's another—and much more predictable—type of appreciation that can impact the value of your home.

Simply put, an updated home will be worth more than an outdated one. A home with more bathrooms is worth more than one with fewer bathrooms. A home that smells like the inside of a litter box will be worth more once that scent is gone. Unwanted features can cause a property to sit unsold for a long time—and the longer it sits, the more it looks like there's something horribly wrong with the house itself.

However, all these issues have one thing in common: They are completely within your ability to change—that is, if you buy the right house.

Let's hark back to Alex and Shelby from the introduction. They bought a beautiful, updated home that didn't need an ounce of work, hence the painfully high price. There were no weird smells or unfinished basement spaces, and the kitchen was pretty as can be.

Our new friend Erin, on the other hand, found a house that is quite the opposite. (The forced appreciation is strong with this one.) It has three bedrooms and three bathrooms plus an office and an unfinished basement. The original owner, who is now the seller, bought it brand-new in 1979—and was a lifelong indoor smoker. He didn't update the home at all, so it's a perfect shrine to the 1970s: shag carpet as far as the eye can see and a winning combination of floral wallpaper and wood paneling on the walls. And the pièce de résistance? A poorly maintained in-ground pool in a part of the country where in-ground pools are an absolute upkeep nightmare.

This property made its debut on the market with a higher asking price because the original owner kept the place in decent shape. It sat untouched for a month before being pulled and relisted at a more reasonable price—$175,000 less than what a (much nicer and pool-less) home around the corner had sold for six months earlier.

While Erin's home will need a lot of work to bring it up to the same standards as the neighboring home with the same floor plan, she has a good idea how much appreciation she can realize, since the neighbor's similar home sold for $175,000 more. Even if she has to spend $50,000 on the rehab, that still leaves her with more than $100,000 in profit.

While most first-time home buyers won't have the skills, money, or network to pull off a massive renovation project, that doesn't mean all is lost. First, you don't have to buy a full-gut rehab that reeks of smoke and hasn't been updated in forty years in order to take advantage of forced appreciation. Second, there's plenty you can do short of total rehab to increase the value of a home. A fresh coat of paint can transform a room. Flooring is relatively inexpensive and easy to install (or have installed). Replacing outdated fixtures—from doorknobs to ceiling fans to outlet covers—can change the entire look of an older home.

The more someone is willing to take on reasonable DIY efforts—and the more they understand how those improvements will impact their property's value—the better. Compared to Alex and Shelby, who chose to buy at a high price point, Erin is putting herself in a better position to add value to her home. Not only was the outdated home itself a smart choice, but with plenty of padding in her financial position, Erin will be less intimidated by doling out cash for a renovation project.

If you want to follow in Erin's footsteps, a good starting point is to look for a property that needs paint, new bathroom vanities, and a yard makeover. You should stay away from anything too crazy (like knocking down walls, unless you're into that sort of thing), but don't underestimate what a little elbow grease can accomplish.

Even if you're about as handy as a cactus wearing a toolbelt, the internet is positively brimming with step-by-step tutorials. All the big-box home improvement stores offer classes on various home improvement skills that you can learn using *their* equipment and supplies. YouTube has a video for every repair under the sun. If all else fails—or if you're an old soul—physical, real-life libraries have reference books filled with step-by-step illustrations and instructions.

If you're willing to take on a little more work, certain projects will get you more bang for your buck. As fun as it might be to add a home theater in the basement, some projects cost more than they will recoup with the home's resale value. Most often, the best value-add renovations are:

- **Bathroom remodel.** On average, a bathroom remodel costs about $10,000, depending on how fancy you want to get. With some clever DIY work, you might be able to pull off a budget of $5,000 for a smaller bathroom.

- **Kitchen remodel.** Though even a minor kitchen remodel rings in at a hefty $20,000, it's one of the universal ways to add value to a home. Who wouldn't want new countertops, shiny appliances, and those fancy soft-closing drawers? Depending on how ugly the kitchen is before remodeling, this project might be a no-brainer to add massive value to the home.

- **Adding square footage.** This is more costly and labor-intensive, but by adding square footage to a home—by, for example, constructing a bedroom in the attic or adding a bathroom in the basement—you instantly jack up the home's value. A two-bedroom, two-bathroom house is worth a lot less than a three-bedroom, three-bathroom house, no doubt about it. Note that these features must conform to certain laws to be considered "real" bedrooms and bathrooms, however, which is key to recouping the cost of the project.

- **Interior paint.** Yes, this makes the list. Why? Because it's so cheap that it's basically a no-brainer. A gallon of paint costs about $30, and a just few gallons can change the entire look of the home. Try to stick to more neutral colors for the best resale value.

- **New flooring.** The cost of this project can vary wildly depending on what materials you choose, and the value it will add depends on what type of flooring you're replacing. If you're able to upgrade stained carpet to something like laminate flooring, you're adding big bucks to that home's value. Some old homes have hardwood *under* the carpet, though there's no guarantee it will be in good shape. If you're able to refinish pre-existing hardwood, that's much cheaper than putting in new floors.

- **Landscaping and exterior paint.** It's all about curb appeal. Again, the cost of these projects varies depending on the lot size and type of home, but they usually are worth what they cost. The face of your home is what will attract buyers, and curb appeal is touted as an important feature for sellers and buyers alike.

By looking for an outdated home, you are choosing a different path than most of your peers. Most buyers react emotionally to a home's appearance. They're looking for perfection, and they want it now. They turn up their noses at walls that are painted anything but muted, agreeable gray. They won't even look at flooring unless it's polished, dark-stained hardwood. With an open mind and an eye toward the future, you can best their short-sightedness with a healthy dose of forced appreciation. Purchase that otherwise unwanted house at a discount, and turn it into the beauty that everyone wanted it to be. You'll enjoy significant savings when you buy—and a huge bonus when you sell.

# APPRECIATION AND TAXES

Bear with us, because this section may be...taxing.

If you survived that joke without putting down this book, congratulations! You appreciate us, we appreciate you, and now you get a great appreciation tip: Building home equity can be an extremely tax-advantaged way to build wealth. The IRS has a rule by which you can exclude up to $250,000 of capital gains from the sale of your home as an individual, and up to $500,000 on the sale of your home as a married couple.

What does that mean? If you experience a combination of market and forced appreciation and you're sitting on a big chunk of change, then—wait for it—you don't have to pay taxes on that gain when you sell your home.

There are rules, of course. You must have lived in the property as a primary residence for two or more of the last five years—so it can't be rented out to others for five years straight, and it can't be a house that you flip for profit with a quick turnaround time. If you follow these rules, you're in a good spot to make tax-free money on the sale of your home.

This may sound like a trap, but it's actually the basis of a specific investing strategy called the *live-in flip*. In essence, the investor fixes up a house that they live in for more than two years; then they sell the home without paying any taxes on that gain. Mindy has completed ten such successful exits from her primary residence with a tax-free capital gain each time.

There is a saying, however, that you shouldn't "let the tax tail wag the dog"—basically, don't make a financial decision based solely on its tax implications. You never want to make a poor economic choice just to save money on your taxes, but you should still be aware of the rules related to selling or keeping your property. For example, it would be a shame to buy a home, improve it, live there for one year and ten months, then move out and sell it. If Erin from our previous example did this with her renovated home, that $125,000 gain in property value could cost her up to $40,000 in taxes when selling the property.

The same applies to renting the property. You buy a house, improve it, live there for a few years, move out, keep it as a rental property for four years, and *then* try to sell it. That's one year too many as a rental property, and that one year can cost you tens of thousands of dollars in taxes.

When it comes to the decision to sell or rent your home, a consultation with a knowledgeable CPA may help you make, or keep, a massive amount of money. Don't let the tax tail wag the dog, but don't chop off the tail, either. (Unless you are a highly trained and trustworthy veterinary professional.)

# CHAPTER SUMMARY

- Appreciation is the increase in a property's value over time. The appreciation cake comes in two flavors—market and forced—and you should aim for a home that has high potential for both.
- The national average for market appreciation is about 3.4 percent, but this can vary greatly depending on regional and local factors. Understand your local market, and keep your eyes peeled around the house you want to buy to avoid any unpleasant surprises after you move in.
- Don't buy the best house in the best neighborhood, which leaves little room for appreciation. Instead, go for the worst house in the best neighborhood—or, at least, the worst house you feel comfortable with.

- Forced appreciation is when you make an ugly house not so ugly. Not only do you spend less on the house because it is less desirable, but you can fix it up and get a big cash bonus from all that equity. Just make sure the projects you take on are worth their weight in added value.
- Don't forget about every person's favorite thing: *taxes!* (Did you flinch?) If you live in a property as a primary residence for two or more of the last five years, you can exclude up to $250,000 in capital gains tax as an individual—or $500,000 as a married couple—on the sale of that home.

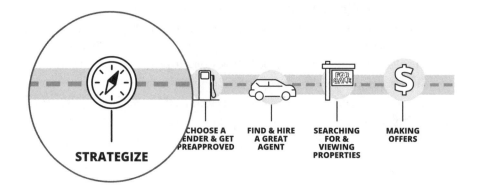

STRATEGIZE — CHOOSE A LENDER & GET PREAPPROVED — FIND & HIRE A GREAT AGENT — SEARCHING FOR & VIEWING PROPERTIES — MAKING OFFERS

CHAPTER FOUR

# ANALYZING RENTAL OPPORTUNITIES

Just when you think things couldn't get more complicated, we throw real estate investing at you. Though it sounds intimidating, what we'll talk about here is actually quite simple. Anyone can do it, and by taking that scary leap into the world of investing, you'll be miles ahead of your more traditional peers.

We're the first to admit that we, the authors, are inherently biased. We've both invested in real estate and have personally experienced the countless benefits from doing so. We represent BiggerPockets.com, a real estate investing and wealth-building community, and have seen people all over the world enjoy the same benefits. If you don't believe us, we won't spend too much time trying to convince you, but there are countless other books and resources that demonstrate the power of real estate investing as a wealth-building tool.

Still, you may not be reading this book with the intention of becoming a landlord with multiple properties. That's fine, but we think that every homeowner should have at least a basic understanding of how their house will fare as a rental. If a homeowner needs to move abruptly and can't sell their house, renting it out to tenants is the next best thing (or maybe even better). History—even the last decade alone—has proved that the basics of real estate investing are essential knowledge for all homeowners, and ignoring this option as a potential exit strategy can impose an expensive limit on your life options.

There are plenty of books out there that provide far greater detail on being a landlord and investing in rental property, and we encourage you to read them to expand your knowledge. This book will focus only on the basics of cash flow in the context of buying a house, since you should at least consider this factor when searching for a property. Just as you should run the numbers for your monthly mortgage when you find a house you like, you should also run the numbers for its potential as a rental down the line. It might sound overzealous to do the math for something you're not even sure you'll take advantage of, but you can never be too careful when putting a significant portion of your life savings on the line.

In this chapter, we'll give you a broad overview of the ways in which your home can generate income as a short-term or long-term rental property. There are also creative strategies that homeowners have used to "hack" their housing to help cover mortgage costs while still living there. Not every tactic works for every situation, but we'll summarize the options that are available to help offset the cost of homeownership.

(When we say "hack your housing," we mean that you might not have to pay some or all of your own mortgage. In fact, you may even *get paid* to own your home. Do we have your attention now?)

## THE NUMBERS BEHIND LONG-TERM RENTALS

A great first-time home purchase will allow you to *cash flow* the property—that is, generate sufficient rental income to cover mortgage payments and maintenance costs—in the event that you move out. Done right, this strategy can result in your rental property covering all its own costs with a little money left over. That money goes right into your pocket, all while paying down your mortgage and building equity.

You already know some of the expenses associated with owning a home from our earlier chapters, but let's dig a little deeper.

## Homeownership Expenses

First and foremost is your mortgage payment, which usually includes property taxes and home insurance. For the sake of this discussion, we'll just call it a mortgage payment. (We'll go into more detail when we talk about your loan in Chapter Six.)

On top of your mortgage, there's maintenance. Technically, this category encompasses small, routine tasks like replacing a toilet, repainting a room, and keeping your lawn from turning into a scene from *Jumanji*. On top of routine maintenance, there are *capital expenditures*, often referred to as CapEx. It's a fancy name for a fancy expense—the price of big-ticket items like replacing a roof, installing central AC, or getting all-new kitchen appliances.

An easy way to ballpark your overall monthly maintenance cost is to dedicate 1 percent of the property's total value each year toward big and small fixes. If you live in a $200,000 home, you should budget $2,000 per year (or $167 per month) for maintenance. If that seems like too high or low a number, that's where CapEx comes in. You shouldn't have many big expenses coming up if you're buying a brand-new two-bedroom home, so you can assume a smaller monthly cost than what is typical. If you live in a Victorian mansion with a thirty-five-year-old roof, you should round up your maintenance allocation to account for the larger expenses that will almost definitely pop up.

You would probably like to have electricity and running water, so let's not forget about utilities. Depending on where you live, your utility expenses will include some or all of the following: electricity and natural gas, water and sewer, trash removal and recycling, and—last but not least—access to the World Wide Web and your portable cellular device. (Although, let's be real. You're probably paying for both of these already as a renter—and so would your hypothetical future tenants.) You can estimate all these costs based on what is typical in your area.

These four make up the holy quartet of home expenses: mortgage, maintenance, CapEx, and utilities. While these are good to keep in mind in general, we're talking specifically about renting out your house to someone else—so there are a few more layers to add to this cake.

## Rental Income and Expenses

If a stranger is living in your property, they will hopefully be paying you for that privilege. The sum they pay you is considered *gross rental income*—not because it's disgusting but because it's the amount you get prior to taking out any expenses.

To estimate what gross rental income might look like for your property, you're going to have to do a little research. The easiest (and free-est) way is to look at rental listing sites like Zillow, Trulia, or even Craigslist. Narrow down your search to the neighborhood you are buying in and find properties with similar features—number of bedrooms and bathrooms, square footage, and so on—and see what they are renting for. You can also use a rent estimator like BiggerPockets Insights—just know that although the data from estimators is usually spot-on, supplementing the numbers with some real market data from your area is always a good idea.

Other than the obvious cost of the dwelling itself, the gross rent will also typically include a fee for utilities. While you can reasonably assume that you won't be paying for your tenant's Wi-Fi and phone bill, you may need to check with local investors or agents on what else is customary in your local market. In most places, landlords will pay for water and trash removal and tenants will pay for the rest.

One more expense to consider is property management. You can manage the property yourself to save money, but we recommend budgeting for a property management service just in case you get sick of replacing lightbulbs down the line. On average, property management will cost about 10 percent of gross rental income. (You might want to slightly increase your maintenance budget too. While many properties will rent without a hitch, you never know when you'll get a tenant who likes to throw potato peels down the garbage disposal...and, yes, that's bad.)

While vacancy isn't a "cost" per se, you should account for that as well. If someone suddenly moves out and you're stuck paying that mortgage on your own, you should have some money built in to cover the absence. This is called a *vacancy allowance*, and it should generally be about 10 percent of gross rent or else the equivalent of one to two months' rent.

Though it may sound like renting out a property is more trouble than it's worth—a life full of lightbulbs, potato peels, and vacant rooms—you might change your mind once we start breaking down the numbers.

## Break It Down Now

If you're a math person, we *figure* you'll like this next section. (Get it?) If you like math as much as you like a glass of orange juice after brushing your teeth, bear with us. We'll start by bringing all the variables together into one equation:

**Gross rental income (including utilities fee)**
- **Mortgage payment** (including principal, interest, taxes, and insurance)
- **Cost of utilities**
- **Vacancy allowance** (10 percent of gross rents)
- **Maintenance and CapEx** (estimated at 1 percent of the property's value, divided by 12 for monthly cost)
- **Property management** (10 percent of gross rents)

---

**Cash flow**

Makes sense, right? Income minus expenses equals money left over. Where does that money go? Oh, right, it's yours to keep.

Now, let's try assigning some real monthly numbers. Let's say you own a $250,000 house that has a mortgage payment of $1,200 per month. You do some research and find that similar homes nearby rent for about $1,800 per month, and your tenants will pay all their utilities (which is slightly unrealistic, but better for the sake of simplicity). Your maintenance cost calculates to about $208, but you round it up a little since your property is older.

Bringing them all together, the numbers look like this:

**$1,800 gross rental income**
**Tenants pay all utilities** (including water, trash removal, etc.)
- **$1,200 mortgage payment**
- **$180 vacancy allowance**
- **$180 property management allowance**
- **$240 maintenance/CapEx allowance**

---

**$0 cash flow**

You might be asking, "Wait, what happened to my money?" That's a reasonable reaction to a big fat zero. In our opinion, a break-even cash flow is the absolute floor that you should look for when buying a home. Anything less than that, and keeping the property after moving out is a losing proposition that limits your exit options and gives you a high risk of being in a tough position down the line.

For example, if you're making break-even cash flow on your rental property, you might be seeing the benefits of someone else paying down your mortgage balance without having to lift a finger (or a penny). It's all sunshine and rainbows until your local housing market tanks and you have to reduce the cost of rent to keep any tenants around. Once that $1,800 rent payment drops to $1,700, you're $100 in the hole. You don't want to subsidize someone else's housing costs out of your own pocket unless you absolutely have to.

Let's try this again with the same property, but in an area with higher average rents:

$2,000 **gross rental income**
**Tenants pay all utilities** (including water, trash removal, etc.)
– $1,200 **mortgage payment**
– $200 **vacancy allowance**
– $200 **property management allowance**
– $240 **maintenance/CapEx allowance**

___

$160 **cash flow**

Now, that's more like it. A great first-time home purchase will have the potential to produce positive cash flow each month as a rental, even if it's just a couple hundred bucks. That might not seem like much relative to your down payment, but that's typical for a single-family home. It's hard enough as an investor to find a rental property with great cash-flow numbers, let alone a home you'd also like to live in.

Your primary residence does not have to be a huge winner from a cash-flow perspective—the goal here is flexibility. The more cash flow your property is capable of producing in the event you move away, the more flexibility you assume as a homeowner. While we recommend break-even or better, we also recognize that even this will be difficult in some markets. In that case, the less negative your cash flow, the more likely it is that you will be able keep your property as a rental should you find yourself in an unfortunate situation down the line.

Losing money each month on a property you're not living in might sound ridiculous, but ask yourself: Would you rather lose the entire property (and all your equity) to foreclosure or just a few measly bucks each month to negative cash flow while continuing to build equity? Although this may not be the best-case scenario, it certainly isn't the worst.

At a minimum, it's important just to know the cash-flow profile of your home. If you decide to go forward with purchasing a home that would be a loser as a rental, at least do so on your own terms!

Like we said before, this isn't an all-encompassing guide on how to rent a single-family property. If you want more advice on how to choose and manage a cash-flow winner, you should check out the other resources we've included at the back of this book.

## SHORT-TERM RENTALS

Short-term rental platforms like Airbnb and Vrbo have taken the world by storm. Think about that for a minute. Prior to the late 2000s, people went on vacation and stayed in *hotels*. What a time to be alive.

It would be a shame for us as investors—and for you as a savvy investor-homeowner—to forget the short-term rental option with your property. This can be a great source of cash flow and even more profitable than the long-term rental option we mentioned above.

There is a catch, however. Many cities around the country frown upon short-term rentals or outright ban them. There are often complicated rules around who is allowed to rent a home as a short-term rental and who is not. Even if your current jurisdiction is A-OK with short-term rentals, you never know when they might change their mind—and you are entirely at the city's mercy.

We're not legal experts, but most parts of the country have been trending toward these tight restrictions. Plus, as the recent pandemic has demonstrated, the short-term rental market can be subject to factors beyond anyone's control. For example, problems with the travel industry could mean little to no occupancy at hotels and short-term rentals alike.

That's why we recommend that you assume your home would be a long-term rental, not a short-term one, in the event that you move out. Once you have a comprehensive understanding of your property's income potential as a traditional long-term rental, you can go the extra mile to see whether you have the option for a short-term rental as well.

The analysis here is similar to the one above, but with a few important changes:

**Nightly rate × number of nights you are likely to book**
- **Mortgage payment**
- **Cost of utilities**
- **Cleaning and management fees**
- **Maintenance/CapEx allowance**

---

**Cash flow**

Finding that first number—nightly rate multiplied by the number of nights you're likely to book—might seem intimidating at first glance. However, the platforms that host short-term rentals often have a large amount of data that can help you easily come up with estimates. (It's their nice way of encouraging you to list your property with them!)

In most cases, these numbers will look significantly better than the numbers for a traditional rental. Make sure you do the research to understand what your home's real income potential is as a short-term rental. If the cash flow is there and you have the time and skills to operate a short-term rental, you have a great potential alternative to a long-term rental.

However, be warned. Lots of people buy a loser of a stand-alone long-term rental just because they think the property has income potential as a short-term rental. Those same people will be in for a nasty shock down the line if they are unable to realize their rosy projections, and an even nastier shock if their city decides to crack down on Airbnbs.

# HOUSE HACKING

We would be remiss if we didn't at least mention this amazing strategy, even though it's definitely not for everyone. More and more people are flocking to what is commonly referred to as *house hacking* in order to offset their housing costs.

The idea behind house hacking is to generate rental income while you live in a property to cover part or all of the mortgage payment. There are many ways to do this, all of which exist on a lifestyle–cost spectrum. On one end, you can purchase a duplex, triplex, or fourplex and rent out the extra units while living in one—the more expensive but more luxurious option. Somewhere in the middle, there's purchasing a property with an additional dwelling unit (ADU), like a mother-in-law suite or an apartment above the garage, then renting that extra space out to a tenant. On the opposite end of the spectrum, you can rent out one of the rooms of your personal home.

Hey, remember when you had a roommate? What about those upstairs neighbors that stomped around like clumsy baby elephants? Yes, house hacking is a throwback to apartment living, but the benefits often outweigh the negatives. When you rent out that extra space (whatever the space may be), the tenant's rent payment covers some or all of your mortgage.

Just ask yourself: Would you trade the privacy of single-family living for a chance to pay close to $0 per month to live in your home? Some might answer with a very stern no. Some might answer with an enthusiastic, shouted-from-the-rooftops *yes!* It's all about personal preference.

We won't go into too much detail here, since there are other books and countless online resources dedicated entirely to house hacking. But we will say this: This weird little strategy has kickstarted many wealth-building journeys, and it's worth considering if you want to take a few baby steps into the world of real estate investing. With house hacking, you can generate enough cash flow to live entirely for free (and then some).

Prior to writing this book, Scott house hacked various duplexes around Denver for seven years. The savings on rent, plus the wealth built through investing those savings in rentals and other investments, currently pay for his housing costs outright. This allows him to *rent* (yes, rent) a very nice condo that is paid for entirely by investment income!

## WHEN THE NUMBERS GET TOUGH...

...the tough get numbers. Wait, what?

So far, this chapter has been optimistic at the very least. Finding a house within your budget that meets your lifestyle expectations is hard enough. What if finding a house with reasonable income potential just isn't possible?

Rather than throwing your hands in the air in frustration and settling for a mansion in Pleasantville, you might want to look instead for more creative opportunities to add value. For example:

- If you are confident that you can improve a property by way of substantial updates, that home's value and rental rates will increase once those updates are complete. (But hopefully you are very, very confident in your DIY skills. Please don't start knocking down walls for fun and then blame it on us.)
- If you can add livable space to a house—by adding bedrooms or bathrooms or finishing out attic or basement space—that can also result in higher home values and higher rental rates.
- If a property is in a location that is welcoming to short-term rentals—with government policy that indicates this is likely to continue—you can generate dependable income after you move out. (But remember: Ye be warned of the allure of short-term rentals.)
- Maybe there's a hyper-local factor that can influence your finances. For example, there is incredibly high demand in Annapolis, Maryland, for short-term rentals every year around the time of the U.S. Naval Academy's graduation ceremonies. Many residents are able to make a significant profit by timing their annual vacations around this major event. They offset one or more full months of mortgage payments with short-term rental income just from a handful of weekends.

Long story short, don't be a quitter. These are just a few examples of how you can put on your thinking cap and outsmart what might look like a tricky housing market. Think of it like having nothing in your pantry but black beans, peanut butter, stale bread, and ramen: Creativity can go a long way.

# CHAPTER SUMMARY

- While you're not obligated to use your property to produce income, you can only benefit from having the option to do so. It makes a wonderful exit option in case you're in a pinch and need to move out—or you can use this option strategically as a method to start building wealth.
- When considering using your home as a long-term rental, you should aim for positive cash flow or at least break-even numbers. If the numbers are slightly less than break-even, know that you are at risk of subsidizing someone else's lifestyle in the event that you

can't sell your property but need to move out. Make sure to do your research and estimate the numbers as accurately as possible.

- Be wary of using your home as a short-term rental. Though it can generate much more cash flow than a long-term rental, a short-term rental is also at the mercy of your city, your county, and how the travel industry is doing. (We're looking at you, COVID-19.)
- Consider creative strategies like house hacking to subsidize your monthly mortgage payments. You might be able to live for free and even make a little extra cash on the side.
- If you want a closer look at real estate investing strategies and how they can supercharge your wealth, check out the BiggerPockets resources included at the back of this book. (Real estate investing is kind of our thing.)

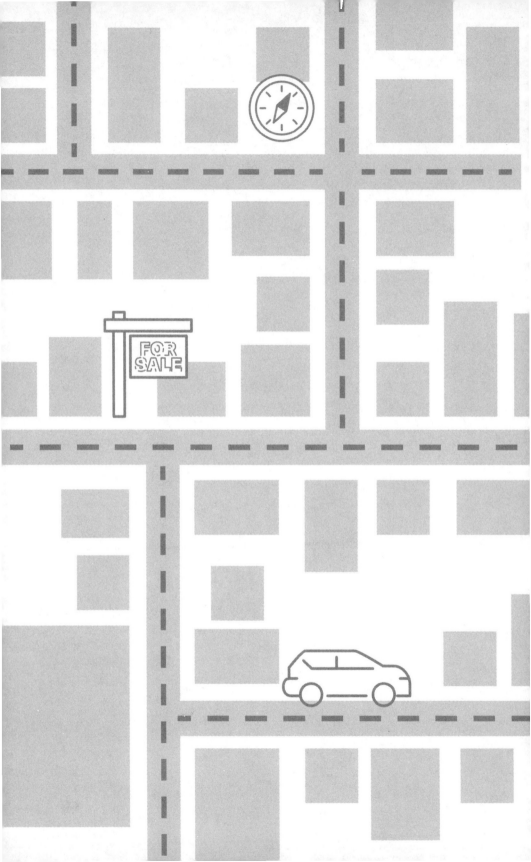

PART TWO

# BEFORE YOU BUY

*"Proper prior preparation prevents piss-poor performance."*

—YOUR HIGH SCHOOL FOOTBALL COACH, PROBABLY

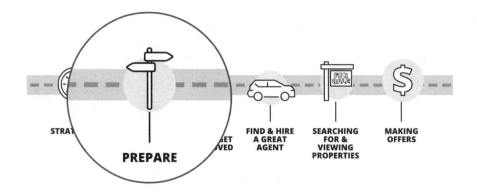

STRAT...
...ET
...VED
PREPARE
FIND & HIRE
A GREAT
AGENT
SEARCHING
FOR &
VIEWING
PROPERTIES
MAKING
OFFERS

CHAPTER FIVE

# PREPARING TO PURCHASE

At this point, you've probably decided whether or not you want to buy a house. You have taken a look at your current housing situation and the local market you live in, and you're better prepared to assess exit options when considering a home purchase. You know how to run the numbers, and you know when those numbers are good.

You have also probably thought to yourself, *Ugh, buying a house is hard.*

The good news is you're one-third of the way through this book, and you've made it through some of the more difficult concepts like appreciation and investment cash flow. The bad news is it's time to get personal and talk about your credit score and savings account. We couldn't put it off forever, could we?

To have the best odds of success when purchasing a home, you need to set yourself up in all the right ways. Finding a great home and buying it at the best possible price is all about laying the groundwork for that purchase. Because good deals are often gone within a few days of being listed, you need to prepare to act immediately when that perfect purchase pops up. There are five basic steps to laying that groundwork, which we'll cover in the following sections.

# BRACE YOURSELF! (AND YOUR BANK ACCOUNT)

Buying a house costs money. What a shocking statement! When you're done gasping in surprise, let's break down the three things you need financially to make this big purchase.

## Good credit

In the context of a credit score, good is typically anything above 700. Great is above 740, amazing is above 800, and basically impossible and literally the highest score you can have is 850. The better your credit score, the easier it will be to access financing and get the best interest rate on your mortgage. While a lender may approve you with a lower credit score, that will then result in a higher interest rate, which makes buying a home even more expensive. If your credit score is less than 700, you will want to develop a strategy that will bring it to 700 or higher prior to your home purchase.

You can check your credit score by contacting one of the three major credit bureaus, or you can use an online service like Credit Karma. (Heads up: Your credit score from a free reporting site won't be exactly the same as the score lenders will pull for your mortgage qualification. Be prepared for the score to shift in either direction.)

The score you see online is determined by five factors: payment history, length of credit history, credit utilization, recent inquiries, and credit diversification. Of these factors, payment history makes up the largest portion of your score—a total of 35 percent—which means that when your payments are late or missed, your score takes a nosedive. Though you can't go back and change the past, you can catch up on any still-missing payments, and you can make all your payments on time going forward.

Another large portion of the overall score is your credit utilization, which rings in at 30 percent. The more you use your available line of credit, the lower your score will be. If you have a credit card with a $5,000 line of credit and a $4,000 balance, one quick way to improve your score would be to pay down that balance as much as possible. Another quick fix could be to request a credit line increase from that same card, though it's much better to work on paying the balance down—and keeping it down.

Let's talk about that for a minute—a whopping 65 percent of your credit score is determined by your ability to make payments on time and not max out your cards. If your credit score looks gloomy, you should examine these two items and work to change your habits. Setting up a recurring reminder on your phone or automatic payments can keep you on track to pay down your balances, which will increase your score more quickly than anything else.

When you're financially ready to buy a home, you should also avoid applying for new credit cards or incurring any other debt—like a car loan, student loan, or personal loan—in the months leading up to your mortgage application. Any new debt can throw off your score by affecting both your average length of credit history and recent inquiries, so try to avoid that double whammy at all costs. We've seen far too many people destroy their loan application with a large purchase right before closing. Wait until the house is yours before making any big purchases.

## Stable Income

In order to access a mortgage loan, you will also need to show your lender that you have relatively stable income. Often, this means income from the same line of work that is visible for at least two consecutive years on your tax return.

While it's fine for an accountant to move from one company to another, that same accountant might have trouble qualifying for a home loan if they instead quit their job to pursue their lifelong dream of being a professional paint-color namer. A change in industry can be tricky, especially if it has happened within the last six to twelve months. (But who wouldn't want to come up with names for fifty different shades of white? Cream of the Crop, Alabaster Daisy, Don't Cry Over Spilled Milk...)

Self-employment and career changes are exciting, but lenders prefer boring. If you're thinking about buying a home and simultaneously making any big moves with your career or personal debt, it's best to have an ongoing relationship with your lender. While most people with standard W-2 jobs will commonly shop rates and go with whichever lender offers the lowest one, folks with unusual or irregular income may want to focus on working with lenders that are willing to work with their situation.

## Understanding Debt-to-Income Ratio

One more thing a mortgage lender will look at is how your debt and income stack up against each other. Although income is important, it doesn't mean much to a lender if it's all eaten up by other loan payments.

Debt-to-income (DTI) ratio is calculated by dividing all minimum monthly debt payments by monthly gross income, and it offers a snapshot of the overall health of your finances. Note that this includes only *debt* payments, such as any loans and current rent or mortgage payments. It doesn't include regular expenses like groceries, gas, or utilities.

Let's say Melissa currently pays $1,600 per month in rent, plus she's required to pay a minimum of $200 per month toward her auto loan and $300 per month toward student loans. That's a total of $2,100 in monthly debt payments. If her annual salary is $50,000 before taxes, that's $4,167 per month—so her debt-to-income ratio would be just over 50 percent.

This isn't great news for Melissa. Though the required DTI ratio varies depending on the lender and loan type, 50 percent is typically considered the maximum for many conventional loans. Melissa is currently right on the fence of an acceptable DTI ratio, and there's not much she can do to change this in the short term—she will either need to make more money or reduce her monthly debt in order to affect this number. At this point, she might need to reassess her financial situation before starting the home-buying process.

The same goes for anyone with a DTI ratio near or higher than 50 percent—you should pay down any current debt as much as possible before applying for a mortgage. However, if you run the numbers and you have a DTI ratio of 45 percent or less, you're on the right track. Make sure to maintain this number by avoiding taking on any more debt before you close on your home!

## Accessible Cash

Moolah. Dough. Cheddar. Bucks. Call it what you will, but you absolutely need it to buy a house.

We argue for a conservative cash position prior to closing on your first home. For us, this means that you have cash on hand for the down payment, all closing costs, any anticipated repairs you'll need to make (if applicable), plus a $10,000–$15,000 cushion left over. That sounds like a massive cushion, but it's far better than having $0 left in the bank the day you move into your new home.

With a typical $300,000 home purchase, this would look like:

- A down payment anywhere from 3 percent to 20 percent of the total loan, depending on the type of loan you're going with. We'll talk about those details more in Chapter Six, but for this example, just know that the down payment could be anywhere between $9,000 and $60,000.
- Closing costs, which come out to about 2 to 5 percent of the total loan. In this example, that's anywhere between $6,000 and $15,000.
- A cash reserve of at least $10,000 after all is said and done.

That means the total amount of cash needed to responsibly purchase this property would be anywhere from $25,000 to $85,000, depending on the size of the down payment. Ouch.

Though you can get creative with your down payment strategy and err on the side of 3 percent, you'll still need *some* money saved up before you buy a home. There are, unfortunately, no shortcuts here. If you don't have the cash in the bank (or stuffed under your mattress), you should start saving up before you go forward with purchasing a home. You're not doing yourself any favors by starting such an important chapter in your life without the funds to do so.

## CREATE AN APPROPRIATE TIMELINE

It's the first of June, and Tyler is considering buying his first home. His current apartment lease is up at the end of July, so he approaches his real estate agent and declares that he needs to purchase a property no later than that move-out deadline.

His agent is delighted to hear this, as it means he's a motivated buyer with a strict deadline—which means sure business. They view properties back-to-back for a few weeks, and Tyler is able to find a property, make an offer, and go under contract with just enough time to close before his lease is up.

That's a pretty standard transaction, right? Your typical middle-class American is usually delighted by such an outcome. However, Tyler made one crucial mistake: He created a false deadline for himself, effectively rushing into the largest financial decision of his life.

"False deadline?" you ask. "But his lease expired at the end of July! He *had* to buy before then, otherwise..."

Hold up. The fact that Tyler's lease was about to expire should have had nothing to do with his decision of when and how to purchase his first property. Instead, he should have created a situation in which *he* was in control of the timeline.

The easy solution in this scenario would have been to go on a month-to-month lease. It might sound crazy and expensive, but too many people make the mistake of timing a home purchase around another life deadline—like moving to a new city, selling a previous home, or getting married.

Remember, Tyler is making a choice that's easily worth more than $300,000. Small mistakes or hasty decisions can have five-figure consequences in the immediate future and even more significant consequences over time. Rushing due to an artificial timeline can incur multiple unnoticeable "soft" costs, like offering a few thousand dollars more than necessary in order to submit a winning bid on a house.

Instead, Tyler needs to sit back, relax, and ask his landlord for a month-to-month extension on his lease. Landlords will almost always agree to this—for a small increase in rent, of course, but nothing so large that it outweighs the cost of potential hasty home buyer mistakes. Even if Tyler's rent increases $200 per month, that would cost a total of $2,400 per year, which pales in comparison to that $300,000 price tag. Plus, he probably won't need a whole year to purchase his new home.

Life events shouldn't affect your purchase decision. Always create a timeline where you are in command. While it won't guarantee you a good deal, it will certainly help you avoid a bad one.

## KNOW WHAT YOU WANT

After driving around a few neighborhoods and keeping a diligent eye on listing platforms like Zillow, Redfin, and the MLS (which you can access through a real estate agent) you should start to form an understanding whether the types of properties you want to buy—and those that meet your financial goals—actually exist. It's your job, not your real estate agent's, to determine what you want and whether those wants are realistic.

Let's say that again. It is *your* job—not your real estate agent's—to determine what you want and whether those wants are realistic. You are the one who will be living there, and you are the one who will be paying the mortgage. Your agent can help guide you toward homes that fit the parameters you have set up, but your agent should not be deciding what you want.

In order for your agent to help you transact on the right house, you will need a crystal-clear definition of what kind of purchase you are willing to make. Plus, the more you know in advance, the less likely you are to be distracted by a feature in an otherwise unsuitable home. (As much as we love smart lights and phone-charging stations, they probably aren't a top priority.)

You should consider the following:

## What is the maximum price you're willing to pay for a home?

To help with this, take your price and run it through a mortgage calculator. This will give you an idea of the monthly payment you would be making on a home at that price. Make sure you also include home insurance, property taxes, and any extra fees like private mortgage insurance (PMI, which we'll explain in Chapter Six) when estimating your monthly cost.

## How much house do you need?

Of course, you should know how many bedrooms and bathrooms you're looking for, and we strongly recommend having at least two toilets. (In addition to the obvious disadvantages, a home with only one bathroom is outdated—yes, even if the rest of the home is remodeled. Houses with two toilets sell faster and for more money than houses with only one.)

Also consider whether you need a home office, basement space, or garage space, and how big a yard you'll want, and make sure you're thinking five to seven years in the future. If you plan on expanding your family or currently have small children, take that into consideration. (Spoiler: They get so much bigger!)

## Location, Location, Location...

Location is the one thing you can't change about your home. You probably know what city you want to live in, but are there other options nearby that may also work? Compare the resident amenities like recreation centers, city parks, and downtown features like shopping and restaurants. There may be better cities for you than the one you're attached to—or if there aren't, that information will help cement your original choice.

Then, zoom in on the smaller details. One thing you might be tempted to ignore is your personal commute time. Though houses might be better on the other side of town, do you really want to spend hours each day commuting to and from work? When considering a home that would add to your current commute, we strongly urge you to drive your expected route during rush hour to see just how bad it will be. If sitting in traffic and spending more money on gas is your idea of a good time, go for it! (If you work from home, the world is your oyster.)

While it may sound irrelevant if you don't have children, buying a house in a good school district is always a plus. Homes in a good district sell faster and for more money than houses in a mediocre or worse district. Kids or no kids, you'll still enjoy the benefits of that district when you go to sell. However, you should also note that a good school district often comes with higher property taxes. Make sure those higher expenses are worth it by looking at similar homes in both districts—at least online—to compare pricing.

Last but not least, some parts of the country have huge floodplains while others have smaller ones or none at all. If your property is located in a floodplain, you'll need to purchase flood insurance, which can be quite expensive. Flood insurance is available only through the federal government, which unfortunately means no price shopping.

## How updated should the home be?

Are you looking for something more polished, or something with which you can force appreciation? If the latter, you should know which projects you're willing to take on. Home renovation shows might be a great source of entertainment (*move—that—bus!*), but the projects on TV are never as simple as they seem. You might walk into an older home and think, *Well, I can just tear down that wall to open up the kitchen. Instant value-add!* Though the idea is tempting, you might regret that decision down the road.

Make sure you consider your DIY skills before diving into showings. What projects might you be willing to tackle to add value to a home? What's completely off the table? This depends entirely on your own abilities, or at least your willingness to learn any new skills needed to execute your plans.

You might be happy to update the paint, landscaping, and appliances but not be willing to commit to any major projects that involve a contractor (like moving walls, repairing the foundation, updating the electrical service, fixing the roof, or any other high-ticket items). Maybe you're fine replacing the floors, but you don't want to deal with windows. Just make sure you know your limitations so you can avoid those items should they come up.

## Do you want to live in an HOA community?

Ah, the homeowner's association. Some people love HOAs and some people hate them. Why? Rules. Lots and lots of rules. Some help keep the neighborhood looking good—so no overlong grass, no weeds, and no broken-down cars in your neighbor's front yard. Some seem overly restrictive, like limiting the number of cars that can be parked in your driveway, your ability to rent out the house should your circumstances change (did someone say *exit option*?), and even limiting the size and type of pets you're allowed to have.

These neighborhoods are also called covenant-controlled communities. They can provide order to a neighborhood and enforce uniformity, and they charge a fee for all this. Your HOA dues are used to maintain any common areas, and while they start around $100 per month, they can climb dramatically depending on the area and the amenities. A neighborhood with a pool, tennis courts, basketball courts, meeting space, playgrounds, and large open spaces that provides trash and snow removal and landscaping can easily reach $1,000 per month in HOA fees. This fee doesn't pay a cent toward your mortgage but is still coming out of your pocket every month. If you are interested in HOA homes, make sure you factor this cost into your monthly budget.

Whether or not you want to live in an HOA community depends entirely on personal preference. If you don't want an HOA telling you what you can do with your property—like the type of plants you're allowed to put in your yard, the color you can paint your home's exterior, and so on—make sure you're not buying in a covenant-controlled neighborhood. On the other hand, if you want the neighborhood structure that comes along with the rules—like no one neglecting their yard or stuffing the street full of dangerously parked vehicles—make sure to tell your agent.

## What features are an absolute must?

Make a list of the things you can't live without, sucn as a big kitchen, garage space, a good school district, and so on.

## What features are complete deal breakers?

Likewise, make sure you write down anything you can't live *with*, like a high-maintenance backyard or being adjacent to a busy street.

Knowing the answer to each of these questions will give you a clear idea of what you want. That way you'll be able to keep your eyes on the prize when you start looking at properties in person. You'll also be able to communicate your needs to a lender and a real estate agent. Here's a great example:

> *I would like a two-bedroom, two-bathroom home in Denver, Colorado, in the neighborhoods of Sloan's Lake, the Highlands, Capitol Hill, or River North. I'm looking for a property priced at $400,000 or less. My home must have a solid master bedroom with a closet, an open kitchen, and a two-car garage, but I'm not interested in anything within an HOA community, on a busy street, within five blocks of a high school, or next door to a commercial property. I will also pay more for properties that have easy access to features like parks or restaurants, and I'll pay less for areas closer to major thoroughfares or industrial buildings. I'm willing to take on a house that needs new paint, landscaping, and bathroom updates but nothing more involved than that. I understand my target neighborhoods reasonably well, and five to ten properties that more or less meet my criteria appear to have sold in the last 180 days.*

This buyer is not living in fantasyland, since similar properties have *sold* in the last six months—note the emphasis on "sold." This is absolutely critical, and here's why.

# DEFINING A GOOD DEAL

It's important not to form your opinions about the market based on active listings. Good deals don't last long in a seller's market, so when you look at properties currently for sale, you're looking at the deals that are either brand-new or have been sitting on the market for a couple of weeks.

Suppose there are ten identical properties that meet the above buyer's criteria, and they'll be listed at the following prices over the next six months:

- $375,000

- $380,000
- $385,000
- $390,000
- $395,000
- $400,000
- $405,000
- $410,000
- $415,000
- $420,000

Now, suppose that over the next six months, six of them sell. If the buyer looks at the market at the end of the six months, what would they see offered for sale at that point in time?
- $405,000
- $410,000
- $415,000
- $420,000

This is what happens when pulling up listing sites for the first time— you see the active listings. The buyer might go for a $400,000 house thinking it's a total steal, only to find out that they're paying $25,000 more than what *would* have been a great deal if they had done their research.

However, if we instead look at all the listings over the last 180 days, including sold houses, a new story emerges. We can observe and analyze the following:
- $375,000—such a good price that it was sold off-market
- $380,000—under contract the day it was listed
- $385,000—under contract in two days
- $390,000—under contract in two days
- $395,000—under contract in a week
- $400,000—under contract in a month
- $405,000—still for sale
- $410,000—still for sale
- $415,000—still for sale
- $420,000—still for sale

This much more comprehensive list tells you that properties of this type are worth between $375,000 and $400,000. The further below

$400,000 that price falls, the lower the buyer's chance of entering the winning bid—because the lower the price, the less time they will have to react. All four of the still-active listings are overpriced or at least more expensive than the comparable properties that have recently sold.

While it's not likely that most first-time home buyers are at risk of mistakenly buying the $420,000 property listed here, the real mistake will happen more subtly. The buyer looks at the market and sees the following properties for sale:

- $405,000
- $410,000
- $415,000
- $420,000

It's been a week or two of home shopping, and the buyer is getting frustrated. Suddenly, a property comes on the market priced at $402,000. Score! It's clearly the best one on the market, so the buyer quickly makes an offer and goes under contract. Thank goodness they were watching the market like a hawk and were poised to pounce at any moment.

That's the critical mistake. According to the previously sold homes, this property was worth between $375,000 and $400,000—so the buyer overpaid by at least $2,000. It seemed like a good deal at the time, but that was only in comparison to the active listings.

Don't let this happen to you. You exponentially increase your risk of being fooled by active listings if you're buying on an artificial timeline, as mentioned earlier in this chapter. When Tyler first looks at the marketplace, he is discouraged by the current listings, which are *very* bad deals with high price points—but at the end of his lease-end timeline, a *moderately* bad deal happens to appear. He swoops in, convinced it's a good deal, that his real estate agent is a genius, and that he got lucky the property came online right at the perfect moment. (And as we now know, this "perfect moment" is one that he unknowingly invented. Better luck next time, Tyler.)

## PREPARE CALMLY TO ACT AGGRESSIVELY

You should be ready to pounce on a good deal—an actual good deal, based on previously sold homes—the second it comes on the market. However, this isn't a type of preparedness you can rush into. Remember, to buy

your first home, you must:
- Be financially ready
- Have a reasonably long purchase timeline
- Define exactly what you want
- Know what a good deal looks like

Take your time to meet these requirements. Once you're 100 percent comfortable with all of them, it's time to hire a real estate agent and make an offer.

The idea is this: If you've seen five to ten properties that meet your criteria that have sold in the last three to six months, then you know that on average, a deal like this will hit the market every eighteen to thirty-six days. That's one or two deals per month.

In other words, you might have to wait patiently for two to three months for your winner to materialize—or it might hit tomorrow, so you need to be prepared now. You need to have your financing set up, and you need to have a real estate agent ready to go. You need to be notified when a property that meets your needs comes on the market, and you have to offer aggressively and quickly when it does.

Think of it like fly fishing—you could get a bite at any time, but you need to be in the water and constantly casting your line so you can react and set the hook as soon as you get a bite. If you don't act, you miss the fish. If you aren't ready to actually make a meaningful offer, you don't have your line in the water—and you won't even get a bite.

In most cases, a deal that is truly competitively priced will go under contract within a few days of listing. While you don't need to drop everything you're doing at two o'clock sharp to see the house at two thirty, you will have to cancel your evening plans to make an offer within twenty-four hours of that listing coming online.

We know it sounds like you're making a very high-pressure decision on the spot, but that's not the case. You've already tied your flies and casted your line, remember? You're making a calm, collected, confident decision about what house you want far in advance. Now all you have to do is simply react when what you planned for all along actually hits the market.

This is exactly how you give yourself the best possible odds of getting a good deal. Put in the work up front, wait patiently, and when you see what you've been looking for, act aggressively. You will feel your heart drop to your toes when you make that first, fast offer, but the rewards will come soon enough—when you move into your reasonably priced, comfortable home and can paint all the walls Don't Cry Over Spilled Milk white.

# CHAPTER SUMMARY

- Buying a home isn't the easiest thing in the world. If you want the best chance of purchasing a home at a great price, you need to prepare in advance.
- First, you'll need to get your finances in order. Your credit score should be 700-plus, your source of income should be stable, you debt-to-income ratio should be less than 45 percent, and you should have a big chunk of cheddar in the bank to cover the down payment and closing costs and have some money left over.
- Don't rush it. If you're under the pressure of a big life event, recognize that you're probably creating an artificial timeline for yourself. If you're on a deadline to move out of a rental, set up a month-to-month lease instead of racing against the clock.
- Know what you want from the house itself and know what a good, reasonable deal is. Pick out specific neighborhoods and home types and analyze them in advance. Make sure you look at houses that have recently sold, not those that are currently on the market.
- When you start looking at homes, consider location-related features like your commute time, the parking situation, the school district, and property taxes. Know where you stand on HOA communities and factor any HOA fees into your monthly budget.
- Once all these things are in order (and you've picked out your real estate agent and have been preapproved for a loan), you're as ready as you'll ever be. Keep your eyes open for a good deal, and don't hesitate when that deal pops up.

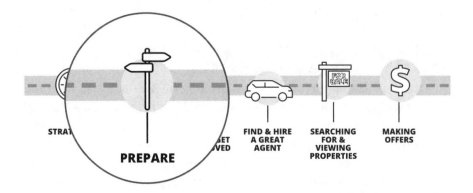

STRA̶̶T · ET VED · PREPARE · FIND & HIRE A GREAT AGENT · SEARCHING FOR & VIEWING PROPERTIES · MAKING OFFERS

CHAPTER SIX

# YOUR LOAN, PLUS A WHOLE LOT OF ACRONYMS

Not everyone is a financial or mathematical genius. If you haven't touched a calculator since high school, we're here to tell you that's okay—you don't need to be a genius to understand the basics of mortgage loans. (And you don't need one of those fancy $200 calculators they made you buy in high school. Psh, what a scam.)

Before we talk about lenders, we should lay the foundation by talking about loans. A mortgage may seem as mysterious as a platypus, but there is a system behind the loan itself—a complex system, but a system nonetheless. Though each monthly mortgage payment is nowhere near as simple as a rent payment, it is made of consistent, predictable parts. By understanding each of these parts, you'll come to understand mortgages and be better equipped to find the best possible loan.

# WHAT IS A MORTGAGE PAYMENT, REALLY?

Your mortgage payment is more than just a big chunk of change to which you bid a woeful farewell each month. When you break down the payment, it consists of four parts: principal, interest, taxes, and insurance. This is often referred to as PITI (and it's a PITI that no one came up with a better name).

PITI is a common acronym used by your future lender. They won't (or they shouldn't) expect you to know all this on your own, and they will break down each of these pieces when you apply for your loan. However, to give you an idea of what you're signing up for, here's a breakdown of PITI and all it entails.

Principal is the portion of your payment that *actually* goes toward the balance of your loan. Depending on your interest rate and loan period, this number will vary—but it's usually a pretty miserable ratio when you start out. More likely than not, less than half of your mortgage payment is actually paying off your loan for the first five years or so.

And whose fault is that? Interest. Depending on your loan's interest rate, a big portion of your payment is eaten up by the bank. It sounds unfair, but bankers gotta bank.

Every month you pay down your loan, the portion going toward interest gets a little smaller—which means the portion going toward principal gets slightly bigger. Depending on the overall numbers, this shift can be a dollar or two each month. It doesn't seem like a lot, but it definitely supports the theory that buying a home is a long-term endeavor. The longer you stay in one property, the more efficiently you're paying down that loan.

We'll talk more about interest rates later in this chapter, but for now, all you need to know is that you want the lowest possible interest rate. The lower your rate, the lower your monthly payment.

The next piece is taxes—or more accurately, property taxes. This number is usually seen as an annual total, which is then split up evenly across twelve months. Lenders require that you escrow your taxes, which means you pay monthly into an account that will then pay the taxes for you. This is because property taxes have precedence over all other property liens, so if you go into foreclosure, property taxes are paid first. Lenders don't like being second in line, so they want to make sure these are paid.

The taxes on your property will likely get higher every year in line with appreciation, but the number shouldn't increase dramatically. This is important to note because if you're using a fixed-rate loan, you might think your payment will never change. While it's true that the P-I part of PITI never changes, the T-I part might shift since taxes and insurance can change on an annual basis.

As of 2019, the typical U.S. homeowner pays about $2,280 per year in property taxes, but that total varies depending on where you live.[5] To give you a taste of this ridiculously wide range, the taxes on an average property in Alabama are $560 per year, while taxes on a house in New Jersey average $7,840 per year. This number can vary even within a single neighborhood, so keep an eye out for it when you're browsing houses. Though this cost seems like nothing in comparison to the rest of your mortgage, a couple hundred dollars a month can make a big difference. Annual property taxes are public knowledge, so they can be found unofficially on any property listing site or officially from your city or county's tax records.

The fourth and final part of PITI is insurance, which refers to your homeowner's insurance. As long as you have a mortgage, your lender requires that you have a home insurance policy. This amount is included in your mortgage payment because—similar to the property tax escrow—you typically pay the monthly cost of home insurance to your lender, who then passes the money along to your insurer. This means you can't sneak your way out of paying it, and you wouldn't want to anyway. Trust us.

The cost of homeowner's insurance can also vary depending on your home, your insurer, and your policy—but just to give you a general idea, the average insurance premium rings in at about $1,200 per year.

Some insurance carriers have made it common practice to dramatically increase second-year insurance rates. If your insurance goes up in year two, call them to ask why. If you don't like the answer, shop around for a new insurance provider. Your lender doesn't care which insurance company you choose, so long as you are fully insured.

# LOAN TYPES

There are multiple loan programs available that you can use to purchase your home. Each one has its own pros and cons, and some have special

---

5  Liz Knueven, "The Average Amount People Pay in Property Taxes in Every US State," Business Insider, September 13, 2019, https://www.businessinsider.com/personal-finance/average-property-taxes-every-us-state.

qualifications. Sellers can also choose to accept some or all of the loan types available, which will be noted in the property listing itself. (If you love the house but the listing states you can't use your type of loan, have your agent reach out to ask whether this was an oversight. It never hurts to ask.)

Though your lender can answer any specific questions you have on which loan will be best, they might not propose something like a VA or USDA loan unless you suggest it outright. Those loans have special qualifications and not everyone—or every property—will qualify. Let's do a brief walk-through of the basic options so you know what's available.

## Conventional Loan

This is the most common type of loan out there. It's the most readily accepted by sellers because it's straightforward, without any hoops for the seller to jump through. Though the typical down payment is 20 percent, you can go as low as 3 percent through first-time home buyer loan programs if you have good credit.

Private mortgage insurance (PMI) is charged on these loans when you put down less than 20 percent, but we'll discuss this more a little later. For now, just know that if you're in a typical home-buying situation and can qualify for a conventional loan, this is likely your best bet.

## FHA Loan

This loan product is guaranteed by the Federal Housing Administration, so there is a lower risk to lenders who offer this plan. That means it's great for borrowers with lower credit scores (even as low as 580) who may not be able to qualify for a conventional loan. FHA loans also allow borrowers to purchase with a down payment as low as 3.5 percent of the purchase price.

However, the seller must jump through a few hoops, and some sellers simply won't accept FHA loans due to the condition of their home or perceived difficulties with the appraisal process. An FHA loan requires an FHA appraisal, which sticks to the house for four months. That means that if the appraisal comes in low, the seller either has to reduce the price or only allow another type of loan.

The home must also meet minimum habitability requirements at closing—like adequate heating and ventilation, working smoke detectors, a functioning kitchen, at least one functioning bathroom, and multiple exits in case of fire. Basically, the property has to be move-in ready. Ugly is fine, but a property that needs a major rehab most likely won't qualify for this loan product.

If you're looking at condos, they are also a touchy subject for FHA financing. The complex must be warrantable—meaning at least 50 percent of the units are owner occupied, no one owner owns more than 10 percent of the units, and the complex is in good financial standing. If the listing does not allow for an FHA loan and you're planning to use one, you need to check in with the seller and the complex to make sure they can accept this type of loan before falling in love with the condo.

## 203K Loan

Aka every house flipper's dream. This is a subset of the FHA loan that allows you to roll rehab costs into the loan product. For example, if a property's renovation is estimated to cost $10,000, then that amount will be added on top of the home loan and paid off monthly like the rest of the mortgage.

There are, of course, a few caveats. First and foremost, the borrower must use certified 203K contractors, which means no DIY projects. This loan is for owner-occupants or nonprofits only, so no investors allowed (unless you're house hacking, since that's just using an investment property as a primary residence).

Plus, there is paperwork—*so much* paperwork—involved with this loan, so it's not the best for the buyer in a hurry. It requires approval for renovation payments, which only come after inspections, which must also be scheduled in advance. However, the obvious advantage here is that the home buyer can finance a large number of repairs and force appreciation that would not otherwise be available.

## VA Loans

This stellar loan program is exclusively available to active-duty military members who meet the current service-time requirements, honorably discharged veterans, and spouses of deceased veterans who died in the line of duty or from a service-related disability. It's backed by the Veterans Administration so, as with an FHA loan, the risk to lenders is very low.

VA loans come with a down payment as low as zero percent—yes, you read that right—which means the buyer is financing 100 percent of the purchase price. They'll pay a version of private mortgage insurance called a funding fee. Also as with an FHA loan, the property must be a primary residence in habitable condition to qualify for this type of funding.

## USDA Loans

This is a fun loan product that isn't keeping up with the times—in a good way. The USDA loan is for properties in predesignated rural areas, and the map that designates what is "rural" is updated infrequently. An online map provided by the USDA outlines these locations, and they're not all cornfields and mountain shacks. You might be surprised by some of the areas that are included.

This loan allows for a down payment as low as zero percent—again, you read that right—and the lowest mortgage insurance and funding fees of all the government-backed programs. But before you grab your straw hat and pitchfork, be aware that you must apply for consideration through the USDA prior to approval. As with many other government-backed loans, your ability to qualify is based on household income, and you must use the property as a primary residence.

## Portfolio Loans

Though they sound like the names of two old-timey radio personalities, Fannie Mae and Freddie Mac are two government-chartered companies that will often buy mortgages from lenders to take the loans off their hands. In most cases, your initial lender will only hold on to the loan for a short time before selling it; otherwise they would quickly run out of money to close on more loans.

However, a portfolio loan is one that a lender keeps "in-house" rather than selling on the secondary market. When a lender plans to keep the loan, the requirements loosen up considerably, since they don't have to conform to Fannie Mae and Freddie Mac requirements. Basically, they can write any rules they want, so long as they don't run afoul of lending laws.

Most banks won't touch portfolio loans. Smaller banks, a local bank with which you have an existing relationship, or a credit union will be your best bet for finding one of these.

# BUT WAIT, THERE'S MORE!

As if choosing among all these loan options weren't difficult enough, there's more to know before you bravely march into that lender's office (or bravely call them on the phone). Once you choose the type of loan, there are a few more options to take into consideration. We could list pages of information on loan variations, but let's stick with the three main loan features: your loan term, a fixed rate versus an adjustable rate, and private mortgage insurance.

## Loan Term

The term of your mortgage is how long you have to pay back the loan. Typically, mortgage terms are either fifteen, twenty, or thirty years, and most people go with the thirty-year option. A longer loan term means more affordable monthly payments, but a shorter loan term means paying less interest in the long run.

Since we're assuming that you'll be staying in the home for five to seven years, you'll want to go with the cheapest monthly payment possible. While a fifteen-year mortgage is sometimes the best option for investors and people staying in their "forever home," a thirty-year mortgage will often be the best option for a first-time home buyer.

## Fixed-Rate versus Adjustable-Rate Mortgage

These two different types of mortgage rates can drastically affect your monthly payments. A fixed rate means that the interest rate of your loan won't ever change. If you sign documents in 2021 for a thirty-year fixed-rate loan, you'll be paying that same interest rate through 2051. (Note that the *interest rate* will never change, but that doesn't mean your *payment* will never change. Per the PITI breakdown, taxes and insurance will still change slightly on an annual basis—and they will almost always go up.)

In our current mid-pandemic market, we're seeing some of the lowest rates ever. Right now and during any time when rates are drastically low, a fixed-rate mortgage may be a smart choice because it's unlikely you'll be able to find a better rate down the road. You'll want to lock in those rates with a fixed-rate mortgage; otherwise, they are likely to increase.

An adjustable-rate mortgage, often abbreviated as ARM, is quite the opposite. The interest rate is not permanent and can increase or decrease over time. You'll see the term ARM with a number in front of it—usually a three, five, or seven—which is the length of time that for which the rate is fixed. A three-year ARM is a thirty-year loan in which the first three years will have the same interest rate, followed by an increase or decrease depending on interest rates at that time.

The good news is the rates on an ARM can't swing wildly. The change is usually only up to 2 percent in either direction each year. The bad news is that can still make a massive difference in terms of your monthly payment, and it's all going toward interest. Depending on the loan amount, 2 percent can mean a monthly payment change of $400 or more.

It sounds scary because it is scary. Why would anyone want an ARM? Well, an adjustable-rate mortgage is lower risk for the lender because they can adjust their rates if interest rates rise in the future, so they charge less interest initially. If you ask your lender for two quotes—one on a thirty-year fixed mortgage and one on a seven-year ARM—there might be a .5 percent difference between the two rates. Those are some big savings.

Adjustable-rate mortgages are a great option if you firmly believe that interest rates will stay about the same or decrease over time, or if you aren't planning on being in the house longer than the initial interest rate period. For example, if you're positive you will sell your home within seven years of buying it, a seven-year ARM will likely be the better option due to its lower interest rate.

While we generally like the ability to lock into a thirty-year fixed-rate mortgage—and we can't fathom how interest rates could go any lower than they are now—please note that interest rates *have* been decreasing for the last ten to twenty years. It seems that every few years a new low is set, and the folks making the "smart" decision to lock into thirty-year fixed-rate mortgages lose money compared with those who select ARMs.

Long story short, a thirty-year, fixed-rate mortgage is the standard for a reason. It's the safest bet for consistent, low payments. Let it be known that we still think a fixed-rate mortgage is the safer choice, but that doesn't always mean it's the *best* choice.

## Private Mortgage Insurance (PMI)

You love to hate it and hate to love it. Introducing your new best frenemy: PMI.

More likely than not, you'll encounter private mortgage insurance in your first-time home buyer journey. This is an insurance premium you pay when you put less than 20 percent down on the house. Frankly, a 20 percent down payment is massive—that's $60,000 cash on a $300,000 house—and it's not always the most reasonable route to take, especially as a first-timer.

If you have the money saved up for a full 20 percent down payment, kudos to you. Not only will you avoid paying PMI each month, but your monthly payments will also be much lower, since your down payment is knocking out a big chunk of the purchase price. You will have less liquid cash left over if you go with this option, but whether or not you want to go this route is a calculation you'll need to make on your own.

If you don't have the full 20 percent, you're in the same boat as many first-time home buyers. Looking back to our previous discussion of mortgage types, you'll remember that the down payment on a conventional loan can be as low as 3 percent for a first-time home buyer with a good credit score, 3.5 percent on an FHA loan, and a beautiful zero percent if you can qualify for a VA or USDA loan.

Those last two don't require a monthly PMI payment, but a low-money-down FHA loan or low-money-down conventional loan most definitely will. With a lower down payment, your lender considers your purchase higher risk, and PMI will protect them in the event that you default on your mortgage.

PMI typically costs between .5 and 1 percent of the entire loan amount on an annual basis. If you're paying PMI on a $300,000 house, that might come to $3,000 per year, or about $250 per month. This chunk of change goes straight to your lender, so it doesn't help at all in paying down your mortgage.

Fortunately, PMI can be removed from your monthly payment once you meet certain conditions. With a conventional loan, the PMI can be removed upon request when you've reached 20 percent equity in the property. If you don't request this from your lender, they must remove it on their own once you reach 22 percent equity.

The timing of this PMI removal checkpoint varies depending on your loan amount, your interest rate, and whether or not you pay extra on top of your typical monthly payment. On a $300,000 loan, for example, you would need to pay down the loan balance to $240,000—which could take ten years or so.

An FHA loan is a different story, however. The monthly PMI-equivalent payments (called the mortgage insurance premium, or MIP) can't be removed at any time during the life of the loan. Unless you pay off the entire mortgage or refinance the loan, you're stuck with that MIP.

Speaking of refinancing, though, this is a great option for those renovating their homes to force appreciation. If your home has greatly increased in value, you might have enough equity in the home to refinance the loan and ditch PMI. For example, if you buy a home with a 5 percent down payment and have seen a 15 percent increase in the home's value over time, you now owe less than 80 percent of what the home is worth, and you can get rid of PMI by refinancing into a new loan.

As with any refinancing, you should be careful about shifting your interest rate and the closing costs associated with the transaction. If you weigh all these factors and it's still worth ditching the PMI, you are off to the races.

### A Quick Word on Loan Points and Lender Credits

A discussion about points and credits may come up with your lender. A point is 1 percent of your mortgage amount that is used as a prepaid expense to "buy down" your interest rate. You should typically buy points only if you're planning to be in the property for more than six years—but they can be difficult to pay for unless you're sitting on piles of cash. You do have a down payment and closing costs to take care of, after all.

Lender credits are similar to paying points, except the other way around. Your lender might offer to reduce your closing costs in exchange for a slightly higher interest rate. Typically, the lender will show you the break-even point (it will take X years for your lower interest rate to reach the equivalent amount of the credit), and it's up to you to decide which is more beneficial to your financial situation.

# CHAPTER SUMMARY

- That was a lot of information and a whole lot of acronyms and abbreviations (PITI, ARM, and PMI...oh my!). To make things as simple as possible, we'll start our summary with this: If you're a typical first-time home buyer with a good credit score and some money saved for a down payment, you are probably going to skip all the confusing stuff and end up with a thirty-year fixed-rate conventional loan. You're welcome.
- A mortgage payment is typically made up of four parts: principal, interest, taxes, and insurance. Over time, the money that goes toward the principal balance increases and the money that goes toward interest decreases.
- Of all the loan types, conventional is preferred by sellers for its

simplicity. There are other options if you qualify for them (like VA and USDA loans) and some for unique situations (like 203K and portfolio loans). An FHA loan is a great choice for those with lower credit scores, but some sellers might not accept this type of financing.

- If you don't put down at least 20 percent of the home's purchase price, you will probably need to make a monthly PMI payment. With a conventional loan, this can be removed once you build to 20 percent equity in the property (through a combination of paying down your mortgage balance and appreciation in the property's value) or if you refinance the loan. With an FHA loan, you must refinance to remove PMI (or technically, MIP—because that's not confusing at all).
- If you're unsure about any of your options, ask your lender for a breakdown of the numbers. They can walk you through which option is best for your personal situation.

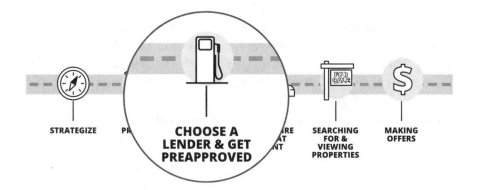

STRATEGIZE · PR· · **CHOOSE A LENDER & GET PREAPPROVED** · ·RE ·AT ·NT · SEARCHING FOR & VIEWING PROPERTIES · MAKING OFFERS

CHAPTER SEVEN

# CHOOSING THE BEST LENDER

Now that we've covered loan basics, it's time to find a lender. This financial process can be intimidating at best, so we're here to give you as many details in advance as possible. To start, you will shop lenders to get a general idea of how much you can qualify for, and you'll use that number to start looking at homes within your price range. Then, once you're ready to start making offers on houses, you'll pursue loan preapproval. With your preapproval letter in hand, you can start making real offers on homes.

You will narrow this list down to one lender with the best possible rates, and that's the lender you'll contact when you go under contract on a house. From there, you will be spending a lot of time with your lender verifying your financial information to get the loan finalized.

But for now, let's start at the beginning. Here are the five main steps that will take you from "Wait, what exactly *is* preapproval?" to homeowner in no time.

# STEP ONE: KNOW WHAT YOU'RE GETTING INTO

For many people, the two biggest influences on the decision to purchase a first home are their lender and their agent. In a typical transaction (which we've already debunked as fallible), a buyer will assume that their price range is equal to the maximum amount they qualify for with their lender. They will then communicate this price to their agent, who will show them properties that are near the upper limits of that range. The buyer is then caught in the trap of buying a house that is beyond their preferred budget, even if it is technically "affordable."

That's not to say that lenders and agents are evilly scheming to get every penny they can from their clients. If you don't know what you want, you're simply at risk of being pointed toward properties at the upper bounds of the price range your lender assigns to you.

Your lender generates income when they originate mortgages. Often, they earn about 1 percent of the total loan amount—so the bigger the mortgage, the more money they make. This means they will give you a very clear picture of the largest possible loan to which you have access. Though they have a personal gain at stake, they're (most likely) not practicing their villainous laughter for the day they triumph over your feeble attempts to get a smaller loan. You, the buyer, should hold yourself responsible for setting boundaries when it comes to the price tag of your mortgage.

Any buyer should go into the purchasing process with a pre-established overview of their true purchasing power, an understanding of their local market, and a strong idea of what they really want out of their home. (Which, if you've been paying attention, is one that offers you flexibility and a step up toward your long-term financial goals. If you haven't caught any of this, you *might* need to grab another cup of coffee.)

If you instead start the purchasing process by talking to your lender about what you can qualify for, you might be blinded by that number because you technically *can* afford it. What could it hurt to look at houses that are on the pricier side? That fabulous loan officer told you it will be perfectly fine to buy that dream home.

The best way to avoid this temptation is to go in with some numbers already in mind. You can use a basic online mortgage calculator to estimate how your credit score, income, and debt will affect your maximum purchase price. Then you'll see what monthly payments might look like, which you can compare to your personal budget. If you approach your lender with these two numbers set in stone—the maximum purchase price and maximum monthly payment to which you'll commit—you can skip a lot of the pleasantries and get straight to business.

Also, it almost goes without saying, but we'll say it anyway: Before you think about reaching out to lenders, you should consider the state of your finances. We talked about the basics of home buyer finances in the previous chapter: your credit score, income stability, debt-to-income ratio, and available cash. If you don't have your finances in order, you may need to put your homeownership dreams on temporary hiatus.

## STEP TWO: TEST THE WATERS

If your financial situation is primed for action, it's time to get started. You're going to contact some potential lenders and tell them your credit score, monthly income, and monthly debt payments. Then you'll ask for a ballpark figure for a loan you might qualify for.

Make sure you are 100 percent clear that you do not want them to run your credit at this time. You're looking for a general figure of what you can realistically afford so you can start looking at prospective properties. You're not quite ready to begin your search in earnest, and you don't want a hard credit inquiry bogging down your credit score before it's absolutely necessary.

This ballpark figure will give you a chance to start browsing homes within your price range, so you'll know exactly what you want when the time comes. At this point, you'll return to the guidance in Chapter Five to figure out what you want and what's a good deal—except now you'll have some real numbers to work with, and you can paint an even clearer picture of your goals.

## STEP THREE: A LIST OF LENDERS

As homeowners and real estate investors, we the authors have personal relationships with our lenders. We value a sense of trust that can expedite the preapproval process, the chance to get on the phone with them, and the ability to make an offer in real time. A great lender in our business can help us close more deals faster, and they have a complete understanding of our somewhat complicated income streams. They'll even point us in the right direction if we need other types of financing.

Finding the perfect lender isn't easy. Lucky for you, a first-time home buyer doesn't need a *perfect* lender. As long as you have reasonably normal income and good credit, your relationship with your lender is much less important. You won't be buying houses year in and year out, so you don't need all the bells and whistles. In the case of a typical home buyer, the situation is much simpler: The lender with the best mortgage rate wins.

Your mortgage rate is the interest rate on your loan, and this little percentage can make all the difference in your purchasing power. The lower the rate, the lower your monthly payment. If a buyer has a 4 percent interest rate on a thirty-year fixed-rate $300,000 mortgage loan, they will be paying roughly $1,400 per month with $1,000 of that initial payment going straight to interest. If they instead snag a 3 percent interest rate, their monthly payments will be roughly $1,250 with only $750 of their initial payment going toward interest. The overall payment is lower because less cash is flushed down the metaphorical interest-rate toilet.

Interest rates can change by the hour, since they're based on economic factors like the bond market and the Treasury rate—but these movements are totally out of your control. What you *can* change are financial factors like your credit score, since your lender will assess your financial situation to determine how risky the loan is. The higher the risk, the higher the mortgage rate.

Interest rates vary from lender to lender, so it's important to shop around to make sure you're getting the best rate possible. APR and closing costs can vary dramatically from lender to lender, so you should start by making a list of multiple lenders so you can ask each what their rates are. There are three main ways to build this list:

- Ask around. Who did your friends use when they bought their first house? Does your agent have a recommendation? Can any of your coworkers point you in the right direction? Word of mouth is one of the most reliable ways to source your lender, since you get to hear from a real person about the quality of their experience.
- Do an internet search. Though it may sound sketchy, even experienced investors have found their best lenders on sites like online loan marketplaces.
- Go local. Credit unions and small local banks can have surprisingly great rates.

If you pursue all three strategies, you should wind up with a decent list of lenders in hand. Then it's time to narrow down that list to a single winner.

## STEP FOUR: MAY THE BEST LENDER WIN

In the past, every time a prospective buyer asked a lender to offer rates, they would run that buyer's credit score—which means the credit score would take a hit. This encouraged buyers to speak with only one or two lenders, especially if they were starting with an already wobbly credit score.

Fortunately, this has changed. Now you can contact multiple lenders in a short period of time for what is considered "rate shopping." As long as they do so within a thirty-day window, multiple lenders can pull your credit and it counts as one hard credit inquiry. This means there's only one ding to your credit, and this single ding should only cost you five or ten credit points.

Make a plan to contact multiple lenders within this thirty-day window. Reach out to a variety: local credit unions, small local banks, large national chains, and mortgage brokers. With each lender, you'll fill out a mortgage application that includes all your financial information as well as what type of loan you would like to apply for. (See, we told you that last chapter would come in handy!) They will pull your credit score and you'll get a real estimate of your mortgage rate.

After you submit everything they request, the lender is required by law to provide a loan estimate within three business days. This estimate will outline all the loan's information, including projected monthly payments with a breakdown of PITI, the maximum loan amount, and estimated closing costs and lender fees.

From here, you should make a list or spreadsheet to compare apples to apples. (No need to reinvent the wheel—you can use the one we've shared at www.biggerpockets.com/homebuyerbonus.) On each line, include the lender's name, the loan's predicted interest rate, total closing costs, lender fees, any credits they might give you, the maximum amount they'll lend, your estimated total monthly payment, and anything else that is pertinent to your choice. With this information all in one place, you'll get a clearer picture of how the lenders stack up.

Which loan is the best may not be obvious immediately, and the lowest monthly payment may not always be the winner. You might notice that one lender doesn't account for certain things like lender fees when they give you an estimate, which will unfairly skew the numbers in their favor. That's where the spreadsheet helps, since you'll be able to see any holes in the information.

If you need a tie breaker, you should consider what is most important to your personal financial situation. Would you prefer a lower monthly payment or lower closing costs? If a lender is offering a credit, this can usually apply to the closing costs or the interest rate. Would you prefer to pay less cash up front or less cash over time?

After all your time and effort spent on this spreadsheet, not only will you be able to pick the best lender, but you will also be able to rest easy at night knowing you got the best deal possible.

## STEP FIVE: PREAPPROVAL

To clarify up front, lenders will use two terms that sound similar: preapproval and prequalification. The latter is worthless. Basically, prequalification means that the lender will give you a dollar amount you *could* qualify for based on the information you gave them. They don't pull credit or run reports. *If* everything you say is correct, you *could* qualify for this amount.

*Preapproval* is what you want. This means the lender has looked into your financial history, and they ran a credit check to verify that the information you shared is correct. While a preapproval letter isn't a guarantee or a loan commitment, it shows that you are serious about purchasing a home. You can still be denied for a loan—especially if you ignore our earlier advice and decide to open up a huge line of credit or quit your job right before closing—but this preapproval letter is exactly what sellers want to see when you make an offer on a house. More often than not, a preapproval letter is a must-have for getting a house in a hot market.

To get preapproved, you will need to submit stacks of documents requested by your lender, such as your:

- Last two months of bank statements
- Last two months of retirement accounts (401(k) and the like)
- Most recent thirty days of pay stubs
- Last two years of tax returns

This won't be the last time they ask for this information. If you go forward with the loan, they will request an update (like more recent pay stubs and bank statements) after you go under contract and the loan underwriting process starts in earnest.

After all is said and done, the lender will provide an "official" pre-approval letter, which your agent will use while making an offer on a house. This is your golden ticket to the chocolate factory, but you should know that it usually comes with a ninety-day expiration date. Don't be alarmed, however. Once you are set up with your lender, getting re-pre-approved will most likely be a straightforward process—so don't allow the ninety-day expiration date to create an artificial timeline and rush your purchase decision!

# CHAPTER SUMMARY

- Finding a great lender is all about doing your homework. Start by asking around and searching online to find several different options, then inquire about their rates. Lay out all the answers in one list to compare apples to apples and determine which lender is offering the best possible deal. (It sounds like a pain, but you'll thank us later.)
- Make sure you confine any hard credit pulls to a thirty-day window. Otherwise they will count as extra dings against your credit score.
- Preapproval is not a guarantee, but it is a sign that you're serious. In order to accept your offer, a seller will want to see a preapproval letter.

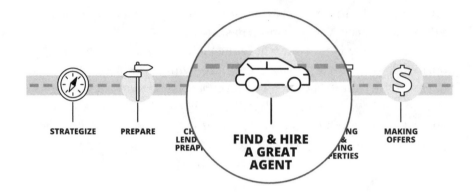

STRATEGIZE PREPARE CH LEND PREAP FIND & HIRE A GREAT AGENT NG & ING ERTIES MAKING OFFERS

CHAPTER EIGHT

# HIRING THE RIGHT AGENT

Unlike finding the right lender, whose quality is basically dependent on the numbers they offer, finding the right real estate agent is much less straightforward. An agent makes money by earning a commission of about 2.5 to 3 percent of the total value of the property bought or sold, which is usually included in the *seller's* closing costs—meaning that you're not shopping for an agent by price. Instead, you're looking for an agent who will contribute positively to your home-buying experience with great advice, suggestions, and support.

To be honest, we've ruined you with this book. You're no longer the ideal client. (You've seen too much.) To a typical real estate agent, a dream client looks like this:

- A high-income individual with a great credit score who's in the market for a luxury, high-end property
- An emotionally driven decision maker who's seeking their perfect dream home and will fall in love with one of the first properties they visit

- Someone who's dismayed by what seems to be a lack of housing inventory on the market and will settle for a less-than-ideal purchase price
- Someone with a tight, deadline-driven purchase timeline

This kind of home buyer basically guarantees a large, quick paycheck. Those who are considered "top" agents are often capable of finding and serving the largest number of these easy home buyers—it's simply good business that means more money in less time for the agent.

You, however, are smarter than the average home buyer. To an agent, you will look like this:

- You have dependable income and great credit, but you're looking for a property well within your means.
- You will have a lower price point than your peers, despite the fact that you have similar income, credit, and savings.
- You are comfortable with a medium- to long-term purchase horizon.
- You know that your expectations are in line with reality, so you are willing to wait patiently for a great deal to come along.

To an agent, this looks like more work, less reward. Many first-time home buyers and investors who share this mindset are perceived as less valuable, which will be a challenge for you to overcome when searching for the right agent. It's important to understand that asking any real estate agent to put in twice the work for half the pay makes you a less appealing client.

Luckily, you can be prepared to set reasonable expectations for working with a potential agent. For your first meeting with an agent, you should come to the table with much of the information we discussed in Chapter Five—like what type of home you want, what neighborhoods you prefer, and what price range you are realistically expecting to pursue. You should bring some examples of recently sold properties that are in line with your expectations.

Then you should demonstrate that you are prepared (both financially and emotionally) to purchase a property and indicate a high intent to do so. You basically need to prove that while you may be looking at a lower price point with a longer timeline than typical clients, you won't be a waste of time. That's your biggest bargaining chip, since it's more than can be said about most clients—even those with a higher price point.

To prove that you know precisely what you need, you can tell your potential agent the following:

1. You want the agent in a series of preliminary meetings or phone calls to confirm—or give you feedback on—the assumptions you're making for your property purchase. Is your research producing realistic expectations, or do you need to adjust them?

2. You need the agent to set up a search for properties that meet your criteria. Because a good deal doesn't last on the market, you need to be notified immediately when a house within your parameters comes online. The Multiple Listing Service (MLS) is faster and provides more accurate information than free online listing sites, and your agent can provide access to MLS listings.

3. You want your agent to wait patiently with you until properties that meet your criteria come online. When and if they come on the market, you then need the agent to pick up the phone, show you the property, and be prepared to make an offer with a fast turnaround time.

Agents will become wary if they sense you won't actually pull the trigger when a good house comes on the market. An agent who conducts twenty showings and submits twenty unreasonably low offers is an overworked and underpaid agent—and asking this of them is not fair. Instead, you need to be ready, willing, and able to make a competitive offer on properties that meet your criteria.

By setting these expectations up front, you're letting the agent know that you need them to perform critical services for you throughout the home-buying process. You're also making it clear that you expect a very reasonable workload overall, since you won't ask them to show you dozens of properties you have no interest in purchasing.

## THE DIFFERENCE BETWEEN PASSABLE AND GREAT

Real estate agents come in all shapes and sizes, and someone who is great for your neighbor might not be great for you. Especially as a first-time home buyer, you need someone who is willing to explain everything as you go, communicate in the way you prefer, and be available when you need them. (And, of course, they should know what they're doing.)

It's not easy finding someone who checks all these boxes, and you're going to have to put in a little work to find them. The best place to start is with recommendations from friends and family—ask anyone who has bought a house recently who they used as their agent and whether they had a good experience. If the answer is "No, my agent never even answered the phone," there's no need to interview that person.

If the answer is yes, you should contact the agent and set up an initial interview. Whether it's on the phone or in person, you should come prepared with a list of questions, including:

## How frequently do you work with first-time home buyers?

An agent who has experience with first-time home buyers may be more aware of special incentives, credits, and programs that can save you money. This will also be the biggest purchase you have made to date, and you'll need someone who will listen to your concerns, answer all your questions, and not make you feel stupid for asking them—even if your questions *are* slightly stupid. (We've all been there, and we even dedicated an entire section to these kinds of questions in the final chapter.)

## How many closings do you handle per year? How long have you been licensed?

While an agent who is not very busy can sometimes be a good choice because they might give you extra attention as their primary client, an experienced agent will be able to handle the many problems that can pop up during the inspection and closing process. When you do find a deal that meets your criteria, you want to eliminate mistakes in the closing process and ensure it runs smoothly.

If you decide to work with a less experienced agent, ask who they work with as a mentor and whether they will have professional help to guide you through the closing process. You don't want clerical errors to cause problems down the line. A professional—even a less-experienced one—should readily acknowledge any gap in their experience and be prepared to turn to a mentor if any difficulties arise.

You can also gauge an agent's experience by sharing your market research and asking them for their opinion. If they are unable to provide the detailed insight that you were able to uncover from driving neighborhoods and digging up recent sales, they might not be in tune with your local market.

After just a few meetings with local investors, homeowners, and agents, you will be able to readily pick up who does and does not know what they're talking about. An agent who is a real pro will show you where you're right and wrong in ways that are clear to you. Be wary of the agent who overwhelms you with numbers and data you can't easily follow. Do not be intimidated by their expertise—instead, insist that they present information to you in a way you can understand.

## Do you have access to "pocket listings" or off-market deals?

As we discussed earlier, the best deals don't sit on the market for very long. A great agent will know many of the local listing agents in your area, so they might have advance knowledge of deals that have yet to hit the market. This kind of networking gives you a big advantage in the home-buying process, since it may allow you to begin researching certain deals before they make it to the public eye—which prepares you to make an offer sooner than the competition.

If the agent responds positively to this question, try to scope out how they get access to these off-market or premarket deals and how many usually pop up. If they don't have this kind of access, that's not necessarily a bad thing. It's more of a special bonus than an absolute requirement.

Only the best-networked agents will have access to off-market or pre-market deals, and they are likely the busiest. It's even more important that you demonstrate how ready, willing, and able you are to commit when working with agents who have an incredible local network. These top-notch agents won't want the business of "tire kickers."

## How easy are you to reach? What is your preferred method of communication?

Though it seems like common sense, this is a key factor. While you may have a long purchase timeline, you are looking for a very specific deal to pop on the market. You need to be ready to react immediately when such a property comes online, so it's very important that your agent pick up when you call them, or that they at least call you back in a timely manner.

Of course, anyone could easily answer, "I sleep with my phone!" (If they say, "Oh, I never really answer. I hardly remember to charge my phone and live in a bad reception area," congratulate them for their boldness and honesty, then make your timely exit.) A good way to gauge the responsiveness of your agent is to call them to set up a meeting and follow up with an email a few hours after your call. If you get a timely response on both attempts, then you have two signs pointing to great communication practices from your agent. If there is a significant delay, you have a piece of information to tuck away in your decision-making process.

As far as the method of communication goes, some younger agents prefer to work only by text, which is great if that's also what you prefer. However, if you want a phone call and they will only text, that's not going to be a good fit.

## Is this your full-time job?

Many agents are part-timers—at least until they start to generate enough income to make it a full-time job. That doesn't mean they're any worse than a full-time agent, but it does mean they might not be available when you need them to be.

Some part-time agents have a highly flexible schedule at their day job, so this isn't a deal breaker. Other part-time agents will only be available nights and weekends, which is obviously not ideal. Just make sure you know what you need, then find an agent who meets those needs.

## Have you ever had to use your E&O insurance? Have you ever been subject to a disciplinary action by the Division of Real Estate?

Pay close attention to the answers. E&O stands for "errors and omissions," and it is a required type of coverage for any mistakes the agent might make on a transaction. Though one mistake doesn't define an agent, you should be wary about moving forward with someone who has needed to file a claim or has been subject to disciplinary action. You want to work with an agent who knows what they're doing and does it right, every single time.

## How many houses will you show me?

We have encountered many people who say their agent announced they would show only X number of houses to them. This is patently absurd, and you shouldn't enter into a relationship with an agent who does not respond with some version of "as many as it takes for you to find the right home."

### What are your fees?

Real estate agents are usually paid a success fee by the seller at closing, so their payment is not your problem. However, some agents prefer to get paid earlier or charge retainers or hourly rates. If you're unwilling to pay for the cost of the agent, it's best to know about any fees they will charge you up front.

### Will I be working with you or with a member of your team?

While their name is on the big marquee sign, many agents work with a team, so they may not be the person you are spending time with. If that's important to you, make sure you know up front who will actually be showing you houses.

### How many clients do you have right now? Will you have time for me?

With a big, recognizable name comes a lot of clients. Does the agent you're working with really have the time to take on one more?

### Am I required to sign an exclusivity agreement?

Most agents will say yes, and that's not a problem. An exclusivity agreement means that you will work with this agent and *only* this agent—basically, you won't needlessly bail on them for someone else.

If you do sign with this agent, make sure you read the document carefully and either ask them for clarification or get an attorney to clarify for you. In many of these agreements, a success fee is earned when you buy a house. No big deal. You don't work for free, and you can't expect your agent to work for free either. However, if you don't use the agent with whom you signed an agreement, you may still owe them a commission. You definitely want to catch this potentially multi-thousand-dollar mistake before you sign anything.

### If I sign a contract with you to represent me and things don't work out, how do I cancel that contract?

This one is important. Despite your best efforts, you may decide to start a relationship with an agent that doesn't work out. You want an easy-to-cancel contract, not a runaround when you're already annoyed with the person. Try to get this answer in writing.

It might take a few weeks to find the perfect agent, so don't sweat it if you don't find the right person for a while. You don't want to settle for anything less than exactly what you need.

A great agent for a first-time home buyer will be understanding and supportive of your specific goals and timeline for your purchase. They will give you honest, expert feedback on your research and offer their opinion on whether what you are looking for is reasonable. They will be communicative and responsive at all times throughout your journey, and they should expertly guide you through the closing process. (You'll see how complicated this process is in Chapter Twelve. Trust us, you'll need all the help you can get.)

In return for meeting these expectations, your agent may have some reasonable expectations of you. They will expect you to know what type of home you want and to be ready to purchase when they present that home to you. In exchange for the work they do to help you research the local market and find a good deal, they will expect you to sign an exclusivity agreement, and for you to work with them for the duration of the purchase process.

And let's be real: Networking is hard. If it feels impossible to know how to articulate what "good" looks like when hiring an agent, lender, or any other professional who helps you in the home-buying process, that's okay. If your family, friends, and coworkers have very few recommendations, don't panic. Just try to meet a few people in each industry before making your selection. The clearer you are on what you want and the more knowledgeable you are, the better you will be able to assess each of these hires.

# CHAPTER SUMMARY

- Unfortunately, you're no longer the ideal client for a "top" real estate agent. (We're not sorry—we're here to teach you how to best purchase a home for *your* needs. Agents can take care of themselves.) To mitigate this, make it clear to any potential agent that you have what a lot of first-time home buyers don't—you know exactly what you want, and you're willing to pull the trigger without hesitation.
- You need four main things from your agent. First, you want a few conversations about whether your home-buying expectations are realistic. Second, you need alerts from the MLS to see immediately

when deals come online. Third, your agent should be immediately available and highly responsive when you need to act quickly on a good deal. Fourth, your agent should walk you through the entire process and answer any questions you may have. Find someone who meets all four requirements, and you're on the right track.

- Some agents will have an extensive local network to help you get advance access to off-market deals. This is a great bonus, but if you can find an agent capable of this, you'll need to be prepared to be particularly detailed in your expectations and committed to following through. It might not be reasonable to expect quite as much attention or hand-holding from this type of agent.
- Don't just go with the first person you find (unless they happen to have stellar answers to your questions). Interview a few agents and choose the person who is best able to guide you, a first-time home buyer, through this crazy world of contracts and closing.

# PART THREE

# BUYING A HOUSE

*"The way to get started is to quit talking and begin doing."*

—WALT DISNEY

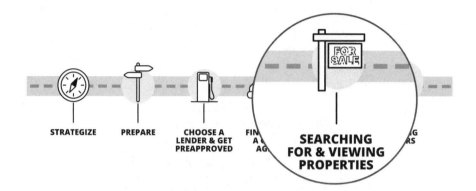

CHAPTER NINE

# LISTINGS, VIEWINGS, AND STARTING YOUR SEARCH

You've prepared yourself in every way possible, but now it's time to actually go out and do what we've been talking about doing. If only it were as easy as handing someone money and—*poof*—you're a homeowner! Well, actually, you *are* just giving someone money for a house, but this is where things start to get complicated. (As if they haven't been complicated already, right?)

If you're unfamiliar with everything that goes into a home purchase, you might leave money on the table or even leave your interests in the home unprotected. The purpose of Part Three is to walk you through the practical side of the purchase and turn you into a confident homeowner with as few surprises as possible.

Your agent and your lender will be two great resources throughout this process. If at any point you're confused or overwhelmed, don't be afraid to ask one or both of them for guidance. They've executed home purchases time and time again, so they will likely have answers to any questions that may come up. (And besides, they're both making a lot of money off your decision to work with them—so they shouldn't be opposed to a stray question, or two, or twenty!)

## SETTING UP LISTING ALERTS

You've found a lender, you've found an agent, and you're finally ready to start checking out properties. This is when the magic happens! After all that time spent researching and making lists, you get to set foot in real-life houses. You never know which house will be *the* one—it could be the very first one you look at, or it could materialize dozens of listings later.

Based on our advice in Chapter Five on defining exactly what you want, you should be able to make three lists that you can send to your agent: must-haves, nice-to-haves, and deal breakers. Sometimes your price range means that you can have it all, and sometimes your price range means you're going to have to make sacrifices. These lists can help convey to your agent what is important to you—and help keep you on track when you see the shiny bells and whistles of an updated home.

Now that you have a crystal-clear articulation of the perfect house—and based on recently sold homes, you know that the perfect house is out there in your price range—you should ask your agent to pull up their Multiple Listing Service (MLS) and search by active properties in your price range. Before you start narrowing down your options, you'll want to see how many are available in your price range alone.

If you're looking at 157 houses to choose from, that can start to get overwhelming—so it's time to start adding your must-haves and nice-to-haves to your criteria to narrow down the options. Bedrooms and bathrooms are a great place to start. (Remember, having two bathrooms is much more desirable than having one.)

Continue to add other items from your must-have list until you are looking at fewer than thirty properties, then ask your agent to set you up to receive these listings via email once per day when you're just starting your search. Spend a few days getting a feel for what is available and at what price, and once you're ready to make a real move, you should change the frequency of your notifications to instantly alert you when a home is listed.

Make a point of viewing your notifications at least every morning and note any properties you'd like more information about. Not all MLS systems are the same, but your agent should be able to look up any address and see whether the home has been listed in the past. Additionally, past listings should have pictures that your agent can review to see if any remodels were completed—which is important for making sure permits were pulled. (More on this in Chapter Twelve.)

Once you've gone through the initial list of properties and chosen which houses you would like to see, set up a time to view them with your agent. Try to narrow down your choices to just a few the first time around—any more than that, and they will all start to blur together by the end of the day.

### A Word on Open Houses

Hopefully, you've been tempted enough to start hitting up open houses in your desired neighborhoods. If you haven't, now is the time to start. These are scheduled periods of time when a home for sale is open for viewing by potential buyers, and they're the perfect opportunity to scope out homes.

Before you get too excited, though, keep in mind that open houses don't actually exist to sell the house. Sure, that's a by-product of the open house, but the main purpose is so the agent can generate more buyer leads. Open houses lead to the actual sale of the home about 4 percent of the time.

When you're there, don't be afraid to say you're working with an agent. In fact, you *want* to let the open house agent know this. If you make an offer on a property, you want your agent to write that offer, protect your interests, and get paid. (Remember, if you sign an exclusivity agreement with the agent, you are agreeing that they will receive a portion of the purchase price as a commission.)

# VIEWING TIPS

Ask your agent to print out listing sheets for each property. Bring your list of must-haves, nice-to-haves, and deal breakers and a pen so you can take notes on any house you are interested in. Jot down the things that stand out in each home to help you remember the property. It may sound crazy, but the homes really do tend to blur together.

If you walk through the house and are getting good vibes, go back to the front door and start looking for things to dislike. While this sounds counterintuitive, it helps you focus on things you may have overlooked in your initial pass because of that fabulous fireplace or those amazing floors.

Keep in mind not just your own preferences but also what a future buyer or potential renter might notice. If you buy this house and try to sell it five years down the road, what could be a turn-off to others? If you decide to turn this property into a rental, what would a tenant really hate to see? If you've walked through the house with a skeptical eye and find no deal breakers, now's the time to pull out your must-have list and look around one more time. Selling a house is expensive, and you definitely don't want to be doing this again in a few years because you are missing features you really need.

Continue cycling through this process until you find a house you like. The process can take weeks, or even months. We spoke earlier about narrowing down your options, but if you're already seeing few options that hit all your bases, you should make an offer right away on a home that you like. This is true in any market, but even more so in a seller's market.

You might see a listing online that looks like a winner, but unfortunately, pictures online can vary drastically from real life. (This applies to houses as much as it does to human beings.) Sometimes the listing photographer will use fancy tricks and lenses to make the cupboard under the stairs look like an actual bedroom. This is a pointless trick, since people will see the house in real life and realize it was all a lie—but it will waste your time. And it will be disappointing. You have been warned.

While finding an acceptable home can take weeks or even months, finding *the* one takes thirty to forty-five days of searching on average. The fewer deal breakers you have on your list and the more cities you're open to living in, the easier it will be to find a suitable home. Conversely, the more particular you are, the longer it will take. There is no right answer—you like what you like, and even better, you know what you want. You've set yourself up for success by avoiding any rushed timelines, so if it takes a little while to find your home, that's okay.

## JUST SAY NO

Not all homes are created equally. If you're a first-time home buyer, you might be tempted to overlook something that will be a *huge* deal to others. This will affect your ability to sell the house down the road, and you want to consider the future as much as possible.

Here are some properties you should avoid:

- **The house on a busy street.** Not only is there more noise and less privacy, but this can be a safety issue to people with children and pets. Don't take our word for it—Stephen King wrote a whole book about the consequences of living on a busy road. (Spoiler alert: The kid dies, the cat dies, the mom dies, the dad dies; everyone dies.)

- **The house near railroad tracks.** Unless you *enjoy* being woken up in the middle of the night by the sound of trains rushing by.

- **The house adjacent to a highway.** If a house is *near* a highway, that could be a potential benefit to home buyers with a commute—but if it's *adjacent* to the highway, you'll get a lot of unwanted noise.

- **The house near high-voltage power lines.** Studies on this are mixed, but some reliable sources claim that exposure to magnetic fields can cause cancer. Whether or not this information is conclusive, a lot of people know about it, and it might cause issues selling the house down the road. (And, you know, better safe than sorry.)

- **The house with a flat roof.** Now, this isn't a total deal breaker, especially if you live somewhere that doesn't get snow. But if your winter looks as much like back-of-wardrobe Narnia as ours does, a flat roof can trap the snow and turn into a disaster. It's easy to forget to look at the roof, so just give it a quick glance before you go inside any house you're viewing.

- **The weird house.** Don't get us wrong—we love a good hideous house that can be fixed up to add value. "Weird" is harder to define, but you'll know it when you see it. Three, four, or even five bedrooms is normal, but once you start getting into six bedrooms, a house turns weird—especially if it has only one or two bathrooms. A two-story house is normal, three is a bit odd, and anything four or more is strange. Just consider anything that you *won't* be able to change with renovations. Geodesic dome houses might be neat to look at, but they're a nightmare to sell.

These are all features you can see and hear while you're viewing properties, so you can nix a few of your options right off the bat. We'll cover more deal breakers later, but those will be the kind you might not be able to pick out on your own. You will need a home inspector on your side, so we'll dive into those when we get to Chapter Eleven.

If you're walking through a home that you realize you aren't interested in purchasing, leave. You are under no obligation to continue to see every part of the house. If there is something you hate or a deal breaker of any kind, simply walk out the door. Crumbling walls in the basement that signal potential foundation issues? A puddle of raw sewage in the backyard? A neighbor sitting on their front porch cleaning a rifle with a menacing look in their eye? Run!

# SELF-DIRECTED PRE-INSPECTION

One great way to save your own time and money is to look out for certain issues before making an offer. It's easy to walk into a beautiful home and miss the older windows that won't open or the bedroom doors that scrape against the floor due to settling.

The following is a long list of things that will frequently pop up during a self-directed home inspection. Granted, a self-directed inspection is *absolutely* no substitute for a professional one by a licensed inspector, but it will give you a better understanding of the house and help you decide whether you want to make an offer. You can also find a printable and fillable version of this list at biggerpockets.com/homebuyerbonus that you can take with you to your showings.

This is a long, extensive list, but don't let it scare you. (Very few of these items are deal breakers, and your agent can help you understand whether any of your findings indicate a larger problem like foundation issues or water damage.) Think of it as guidance if you want to look more closely at a home but don't know where to start.

**General Interior**
- *Windows:* Check that they open and close easily. Look for stains under them, which can be a sign of water infiltration. Do the windows look cloudy or foggy?
- *Doors:* Check that they open and close completely. Do they stick or scrape the floor at any point? (This can be a sign of settling.) Do sliding doors open and close smoothly?
- *Floors:* Any creaking or obvious unevenness? Place a marble on the floor and see if it rolls to check for slant. (Do the marble test in multiple locations in the house.)
- *Walls:* Any holes or poor patchwork?
- *Trim:* Any damage or missing pieces? Animals can be brutal to

wood trim, and matching old trim can be difficult.

- *Lights and ceiling fans:* Turn on every switch to make sure they work. (Note: If the home is unoccupied and the power is turned off, this won't be possible.)
- *Stairs:* Walk up and down the stairs and touch every spindle on the railing. Do they seem sturdy or wobbly? Do the stairs creak? Are any parts missing?
- *Smells:* Has the home been smoked in? Are there musty odors indicating water infiltration?
- *Layout:* Consider the layout of the whole house. Where are the bathrooms? How open is the living space? Does the house flow, or are there walls or angles that don't work?

**Kitchen**

- *Cabinets and drawers:* Open every cabinet and drawer, then close them. Do they move smoothly? Does anything prevent the doors or drawers from being used easily? Check the condition of the cabinet faces. If they were painted, was it a quality job? Is there adequate storage? Do you have enough drawers?
- *Oven:* Open and inspect the oven. Does the door open slowly, indicating the springs still work? What is the condition of the oven?
- *Stove:* Turn on each burner individually to check that they all work.
- *Refrigerator:* Open the refrigerator and freezer doors. Do they open easily? (Note: Exercise extreme caution if the home is vacant and appears to have been vacant for some time. You don't want to stick your head inside a full, unplugged fridge. The smell might kill you.)
- *Dishwasher:* Open and inspect the dishwasher. Do the springs work on the dishwasher door? Check the floor around the dishwasher for evidence of past leaks. The dishwasher should empty into a garbage disposal, so check under the sink for the presence of a disposal.
- *Faucet:* Run the water in the sink. How is the water pressure?
- *Garbage disposal:* Does the garbage disposal run? (Don't forget to turn on the water before you test it.)
- *Hood:* Turn on the range hood fan and light to make sure they work. Peek underneath to check for filth—this is a commonly overlooked area for cleaning.
- *Countertops:* Check the countertop for chips, cracks, and stains. Note what material it's made of, if that's important to you.

## Bathrooms

- *Plumbing and drainage:* Fill up the sink and let the water run out to test for backups or poorly performing drains. If possible, check the ceiling of the room underneath the bathroom for any sign of leaks.
- *Toilet:* Does it rock or is it solidly on the floor? Flush the toilet.
- *Tub:* Any cracks or chips? What condition is the caulk in? Is there mold around the tub?
- *Vanity:* Check the condition. You can check for leaks from all faucets by looking inside the bathroom vanity.
- *Ventilation:* Does the fan work? Is there a window? Does it open and close easily? If possible, make sure the fan vents to the outside, not the attic.

## Basement

- *Odor:* What does it smell like? An overpowering odor can be a sign of mold or mildew.
- *Efflorescence:* Do you see white marks on the cement walls? This could indicate past water intrusion or damage.
- *Walls:* Do the walls have any cracks? Small, hairline cracks are not so concerning, but large cracks—especially horizontal ones—can indicate bigger foundation problems.
- *Floor slope:* Does the basement slope in any direction?
- *Furnace:* Are there any stickers that indicate the installation date? Look at the filter. An extremely dirty filter may signal poor maintenance—both for the furnace as well as the rest of the home.
- *Water heater:* Check for water around the base of the water heater. Are there any stickers on this to indicate the manufacture or installation date?

## Exterior

- *Fence:* Walk the fence to check for loose boards and overall sturdiness.
- *Siding:* What is the condition of the siding? Does it have any rotten spots, missing boards, cracking, or peeling?
- *Roof:* Go to the south side of the house and look at the shingles. The south side gets the most sun, and curling or buckling can be an indication that the roof needs work.
- *Gutters:* What is the condition of the gutters? Do they have

downspouts that direct water away from the home? Do they have any holes? Is vegetation growing in them? Do trees overhang them?

- *Garage door*: Does the garage door open and close easily? Do the safety sensors work properly? Try to close the door and wave your hand in front of the sensor—it should stop the door and reverse to open again.
- *Lawn and yard*: How does the grass look? Are there any dead trees or bushes? Is the landscaping an absolute nightmare? Is this a yard that *you* would be willing to maintain in the future?
- *Slope*: Does the ground slope downward from the home? This is important to direct water away from the home, not into it.

# CHAPTER SUMMARY

- Ask your agent to set you up on the MLS, and narrow down houses within your price range using the items on your "must-haves" list. You'll want to receive these listings via email once per day to start, then immediately when you're ready to purchase.
- Bring your list of must-haves, nice-to-haves, and deal breakers to each property. If you like what you see, start trying to notice the worst things about the property. If you *still* like what you see, use your self-directed pre-inspection list to get a really good understanding of the condition the property is in. And remember, none of this is a substitute for a real inspection—you'll still need an expert's opinion.
- On average, it takes thirty to forty-five days of searching to find a house on which you want to make an offer, but that's just an average. If you are under or over this timeline, don't panic—you know what you want, and as long as your wants are realistic, you should be willing to wait for the right house to come along.

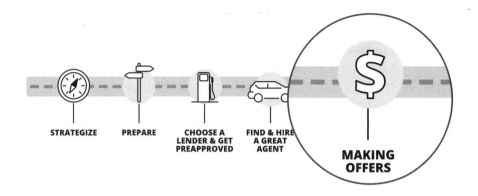

STRATEGIZE PREPARE CHOOSE A LENDER & GET PREAPPROVED FIND & HIRE A GREAT AGENT MAKING OFFERS

CHAPTER TEN

# MAKING AN OFFER

Once you have found a house that meets your needs and you're ready to pull the trigger, it's time to make an offer. Of course, this isn't as easy as calling up the seller and saying, "Hey, just wanted to let you know that we like the house! Can we have it, pretty please?" There will be paperwork, and that paperwork is referred to as...The Contract.

Okay, we're being dramatic. It's not usually capitalized. But this contract is a big deal—it will dictate all the terms of the transaction, on both the buyer's and the seller's side. If you feel strongly about anything, it should be put into the contract. Leaving anything up for interpretation can cause confusion.

If at any point we say, "Put it in the contract," we really mean, "Tell your agent to put it in the contract as they fill it out." Contracts are confusing, and agents know what the various items are and who traditionally pays for what in your area. Usually, the buyer will pay for certain closing costs like lender fees, while the seller typically pays for agent commissions, property transfer tax, recording fees, and so on. Your agent will know all these ins and outs, and they should be able to handle any of your requirements.

Writing the offer can take your agent a couple of hours, so you should be available via phone or text to answer any questions they might have. (As an example, our own state of Colorado's Contract to Buy & Sell is twenty pages long.) When your agent is finally done with their twenty-page-long mental workout, they will then send it to you for approval before it goes off to the seller. The agent most likely uses electronic signature software to fill out the contract, which is editable until someone signs it. It's not so easy to make changes once there's a signature, so make sure you're taking more time to read through it and accept the terms than you did for that app you just downloaded.

Note that most states have "standard" contracts for real estate transactions. Unless you're doing something unusual, this standard contract should apply well to your first purchase. Any meaningful deviation from the standard contract requires an attorney, which can spook the seller and cause friction in the transaction process. Unless absolutely necessary, you should stick to your state's standard contract.

# NAVIGATING THE OFFER CONTRACT

Making an offer can feel like it's happening so quickly that you hardly have any time to think. Take a moment to make sure that you (and anyone else you're purchasing with) understand all the important parts of the contract. We know it's full of legal jargon, but you should read the whole thing.

Without further ado, let's break down the parts of a contract and what each of them really means, so you don't have to spend days combing through legalese to get to the good stuff.

## Parties and Property

The contract will start by defining who is buying what from whom. If more than one person is on the buyer's side, they will be designated as either "Joint Tenants" or "Tenants in Common."

Joint tenancy means you are purchasing with one or more partners who all have equal ownership. This also comes with the right of survivorship, so if one of the partners dies, the remaining partners will equally and automatically split the ownership percentage of the deceased partner. A partner who wants to leave the agreement can't sell their ownership rights without consent of all other partners. This is the most common option for married couples who are purchasing a property together.

Tenants in common means that you're purchasing with one or more partners, but there can be uneven ownership percentages that can also be sold or conveyed to another person without permission of the other partners.

## Inclusions

Inclusions are things the seller owns that you would like to be included with the home—think kitchen appliances, washer and dryer, window treatments, the backyard shed, and so on. Anything "attached" to the home is considered part of the home and *should* be included in the sale—but note the emphasis on *should*. Leave nothing up for question.

You can even go so far as saying "stainless steel Samsung refrigerator in the kitchen at time of showing" in your contract if you feel the need for extra clarity. Mindy once purchased a home and was disappointed to find a mismatched washer and dryer upon moving in. As it turns out, the seller switched them for cheaper models right before moving out.

Learn from her mistake: If you want it, put it in the contract.

(Your lender, on the other hand, doesn't like to see extraneous things on the purchase contract. Appliances are fine, but a long list of other items gives lenders the heebie-jeebies. Make sure your agent uses a separate Bill of Sale for these items.)

## Exclusions

I bet you can see where this is going. This is where you list anything you don't want the seller to leave behind—like that ratty old pool table in the basement, the avocado-green fridge in the garage, or the literal mountain of junk in the backyard.

Don't settle for something as simple as "seller's personal property" in this section, as that could cause confusion. Also, to make a stronger offer, consider keeping this section to a minimum. If you're willing to take care of that literal mountain of junk after you move in, you may be able to use this as a bargaining chip for negotiating the sales price of the home.

## Dates and Deadlines

There will be a long list of deadlines, all of which have confusing names that your agent can clarify. We'll dig into what a lot of these mean (like earnest money, title objection, due diligence, and so on), but the two biggest and easiest are the closing and possession dates.

"Closing Time" is more than just a classic '90s exit-the-bar song by Semisonic. The day you "close" on the house is the day you sign all the paperwork and the house becomes legally yours. This is also when your loan goes into effect, so you should base this on your lender's suggested date by which everything can be finalized.

The day you take possession of the home is the day you move in. Typically, this is the same as the closing date, unless otherwise specified in your contract. In some cases, the seller will want to reside in the home for a period following closing while *their* next home purchase is being concluded. If you are in a flexible position (perhaps you're renting month to month), you may be able to close on your new home and rent it back to the seller for a short period of time. This will make your offer even more attractive to them, which will potentially save you money. Another win for those with flexible purchase horizons!

## Purchase Price

You would think that this, the most important section, would be at the top of the contract, but it can be buried somewhere in the middle, depending on your state's contract. The final sales price of the house can be vastly different from the listing price. This number needs to be high enough to appease the seller and compete with other potential buyers, but low enough to be a good deal. The longer the house has been on the market, the less competitive you need to be. Gauging this perfect price point can be difficult, but you should be able to rely on your agent to guide you toward the right choice.

The purchase price should be based on similar homes that have sold nearby in the last three to six months—otherwise known as comparables, or "comps." You and your agent should look at these comps (including pictures of the interiors to make sure the other houses are as updated as the one you are considering purchasing) and use them to determine the pricing of your target property.

This section in your contract will also detail your down payment and earnest money amount. Remember, anything less than a 20 percent down payment will usually come with PMI.

## Seller Concessions

We're not talking about concession stands, though it would be nice if the seller gave you funnel cake and popcorn after you signed all your closing documents. In this context, a "concession" is an amount of money that you request from the seller to help cover some of your costs to buy the home.

Seller concessions can cover things like the inspection fee, appraisal fee, lender fees, and so on. With these concessions in place, you'll pay less at closing, but you're also turning yourself into a less appealing buyer.

We're way ahead of the game, but seller concessions will also typically come into play after the home inspection. This section of the contract can be revised later if your inspector finds something harrowing and you want the seller to cover the cost of the repair after you move in—think big-ticket items like plumbing, electrical, or foundation problems. Or mold. Or a noxious amount of radon gas. You get the point.

## Earnest Money

Along with your offer, you will be submitting an earnest-money check. This shows the seller you are serious about your offer, and you're willing to put your money where your mouth is. The amount of earnest money will be dictated by the listing, but this number is the *minimum* amount required. If you're up against competition, you can always make your offer stronger by increasing the amount of earnest money.

Fortunately, your earnest money payment doesn't disappear. It's credited toward your down payment at closing. For example, if you write a $10,000 check for earnest money, that will then roll over to cover some of your down payment and closing costs. If your down payment and closing costs happen to be less than that amount, you will get a refund after the house is yours.

Unfortunately, earnest money can be forfeited to the seller if you do not comply with the terms of the contract or if you miss a deadline. Your agent should help keep you on schedule with your dates and deadlines, but you want to make sure you're on top of them as well. Enter everything into your calendar and set alerts for the day before to make sure you stay on top of all you need to do. Though your agent should help remind you, *you* are the one who will be hurt the most if you miss a deadline.

When making an offer, you can present earnest money as a photocopy of the check. (You don't want to actually deliver the money until the offer is legally accepted.) The check should be made out to either the listing agent's brokerage, an attorney, or a title company. Never make out the check to the seller, even if they're selling the home without an agent. You definitely need a neutral third party to hold on to that check in case there is a dispute.

## Loan Limitations

This is where you say which type of loan product you will be using (conventional, FHA, VA, etc.). Make sure you check all the boxes that apply. If your lender can get you a better loan using a different product but you didn't check that box, you'll have to ask the seller for an amendment to the contract to allow you to pursue that loan product. The seller doesn't have to grant the request either, so it's best to include all the loans you could possibly use at the beginning of the process.

## Appraisal Provisions

A third-party professional will perform an appraisal to make sure the home's value and purchase price aren't miles apart. The appraiser will look at comparable properties that have sold recently—the same properties we told you to look at with your agent to determine a purchase price—and use those comps to determine the home's value.

Your contract will likely contain an Appraisal Provisions section, which outlines the appraisal process, who pays for it, and what happens in the event that an appraisal comes in under value. For example, if a buyer offers $410,000 on a home that appraises for $400,000, there are three options: The seller can agree to reduce the price, the buyer can bring the excess $10,000 to the table so the loan amount does not exceed the home's value, or the buyer can back out of the purchase entirely. They should be able to back out and still keep their earnest money if this has been specified in the contract.

Cue the sad trombone. Sometimes a home purchase just doesn't work out.

In the current super-hot market that much of the country is experiencing, some agents are recommending that buyers cover the appraisal gap—meaning the buyer would bring money to the closing table to cover the difference between purchase price and appraisal price. We don't always recommend this strategy, because you're starting off homeownership with negative equity. You'll need to see appreciation in order to break even, which is not a great way to begin.

# Title

Put as simply as possible, title specifies who has rights to the property. When you purchase a house, there will be a title *transfer* in which you are granted ownership of the property and the seller gives up ownership in exchange for selling the house. The title *company* will take care of this process, and title *insurance* protects both you and your lender from any defects in the title. (Though these problems are rare, they can still happen—and if something is wrong, title insurance will protect you against losses.)

If your new home is on a plot of land that once belonged to Farmer Joe, you would assume that he legally sold that property to whoever built the homes there. However, if he pulled a fast one on the buyer and his great-great-grandson has legal rights to half the land under your house, things could get messy for you down the line.

Similarly, if the previous owner of the home never paid for a $30,000 roof replacement, there might be a lien on the home so the roofer can finally get their hard-earned money. If you overlook this when you buy the home, that $30,000 will become *your* problem.

Your contract will probably include a whole lot of title information and requests. You should know who is paying for title insurance—sometimes it's the seller, sometimes the buyer, and sometimes the cost is split half and half. You are also given a few different title deadlines, during which the seller will provide a copy of their current title and you and your agent can scope it out for anything fishy. There's also a title objection and title resolution deadline before which you can point out and solve any problems or back out of the offer completely.

Problems with title arise when there is anything that gives another party a claim to the property. This could be a second mortgage, a lien, or even a previously unknown heir who comes forward with a will that dictates their right to own the property. A lien is placed on a home if the owner owes money to someone and cannot (or will not) pay it. Contractors who have done work on the home and weren't paid can place a lien on the property so that they finally receive their money when the property is sold. The IRS can place a lien on the home if the owner fails to pay a tax debt.

Resolving title problems can be super complex or super easy. A property with one of the problems listed above might not be covered by title insurance at all, or the insurance policy might exclude that problem—meaning your interest in the property can be lost. Title is complicated, so make sure your contract allows you to back out in case of a title emergency.

Once you receive your title commitment after going under contract, read it carefully. You should direct any questions to the title representative and continue asking until you understand exactly what the title document is saying.

## Seller Disclosures

The seller is legally required to disclose any known material defects about a property, whether or not they have lived in the property recently or at all. A material defect is basically anything that will cost a lot of money to repair—like a leaking roof, broken foundation, mold, termites...the list goes on and on.

Sellers are asked to fill out a property disclosure form, but not all states require them to do so. Protect yourself and your investments by specifically asking in writing any questions to which you need the answer. If something is a deal breaker, ask for complete clarification so there are no surprises after you own the property. (Our own personal advice to *sellers* is to disclose everything, since the buyers can come back to take legal action if you don't.)

Fun fact: Death in the home does not always have to be disclosed. This varies from state to state, with some states never requiring death disclosure—even in sensational, well-known cases—while other states require minimal disclosure. If this or anything else is important to you, ask the seller to disclose it in your contract.

## Due Diligence Documents

Unless you're trashing the appliances and mechanical systems, this section is where you will ask for the manuals and maintenance logs for everything. Request information about any warranties on the roof, windows, siding, heating and cooling systems, plumbing, electrical system, and appliances.

You should also ask for copies of previous utility bills to get an idea of the cost to power and run the home. (If your seller doesn't have copies of past bills, they can get them from the utility company. No excuses here.) If your contract doesn't have a separate section for HOA documentation, you should ask for that information here as well.

## Taxes

Property taxes are most often paid in arrears, which means that you pay 2020's property tax bill in 2021. These taxes are commonly prorated at closing, so you will receive money from the seller to cover the taxes for the portion of the year that they owned the property. This should go directly into your escrow account (where the rest of your first-year tax payment will be held by your lender), but you want to make sure you are receiving all the property taxes that were incurred during the seller's ownership period.

Depending on the time of year, taxes may not have been assessed yet, so you won't know the exact dollar amount you will be charged. While it's common to look at the most recent tax valuation and assume that taxes for the current year will be the same, this can get a bit tricky. Because this varies so much from state to state, we are going to slightly cop out here and tell you to ask your agent for guidance on how to proceed. Though important, this should not be a high-stakes factor in the closing process.

## Contingencies

This is a fancy word for "conditions." Most of the items we've mentioned above are contingencies. I'll pay you for the house on the contingency that all goes well with the inspection. I'll pay you $100,000 on the contingency that the property appraises for at least $100,000. If the property appraises for only $99,999, I don't have to continue with the purchase (and I must have a really mean appraiser who won't budge on that extra dollar).

Remember when your mom told you that no one wins with an ultimatum? Well, this is the only situation in which your mom is wrong. Every contingency is an ultimatum, and these ultimatums protect you (and your earnest money) in the event that anything goes wrong during the buying process.

The most common contingencies are loan approval, home inspection, appraisal, and title insurance. Basically, your lender needs to approve your loan, the house can't be secretly falling apart, it needs to be worth at least what you're paying, and there can't be any sneaky clouds on the home's title. If you're currently living in a house that you must sell before buying another, that would be a home sale contingency. If you're moving into a place within an HOA community, the covenant review should also have its own contingency.

If any of these things goes south, the contingencies in your contract allow you to back out of the purchase without losing your earnest money. Those listed above are pretty typical, since they are complete deal break-ers that the buyer should be able to walk away from unscathed.

In a buyer's market, you can include even more contingencies. In a seller's market, not so much. Best not to be too picky if you're up against other people who might start a bidding war on the same house. The fewer contingencies you include in your offer, the easier it is for the seller to accept your offer over another.

Ask your agent for guidance about the market you are in—they should know the sweet spot between protecting your earnest money and writing the strongest offer possible.

Speaking of which...

# AN OFFER THEY CAN'T REFUSE

Grab your dumbbells and down a protein shake, because we're about to beef up your otherwise average offer.

It shouldn't surprise you that the seller wants the most money possible in their pocket after all this is done. Who wouldn't? They also want as lit-tle hassle as possible during the transaction. If you're in a seller's market, writing a strong offer can be the difference between going under contract or going back to square one. (Yes, your offer might not get accepted. Yes, that means you need start all over again—disheartening but true.)

First of all, before making the offer, you should also ask your agent if they can get any additional information about what is most important to the seller. Some will accept a lower purchase price in exchange for speed and fewer barriers to closing. Others don't have any restrictions and are willing to wait for a buyer who can meet their price and terms. If you're willing to be flexible on certain things the seller wants, you might be able to get a better price overall.

Your agent should also ask about any other offers that might be on the table, and they can even go so far as asking what your offer needs to be competitive. While most listing agents won't reveal all these secrets, they might be willing to drop a crumb or two of information.

## Buyer Concessions

You've heard of seller concessions, but what about buyer concessions? (Sorry, it's still not funnel cake.) There are a host of fees and charges for selling a home, some of which are paid for by the seller, some by the buyer, and some split down the middle—think title insurance, HOA transfer fees, closing service fees, transfer taxes, and so on. Can you afford to help your seller with some of their closing costs beyond the typical fees? Offering to pay for some or all of these items can make your offer stand out.

We know what you're thinking. Why not just increase my offer amount? Well, offering more than what the property is actually worth can cause issues with appraisal, which can affect your ability to get a loan on the property. Paying some of the fees that typically fall on the seller will put more money into their pocket without your needing to worry whether the home will appraise properly.

Also, here's a surprise: Money isn't everything. It might be the most *important* thing (nobody lists their house and crosses their fingers for a lowball offer), but it's not the whole enchilada. There are ways to sweeten the deal other than just upping that purchase price.

Here are a few concessions you can make to tempt the seller into choosing your offer:

- **A flexible closing date or possession time.** The more leeway you can offer, the more opportunity there is to seal a better deal. In a seller's market, this is actually quite common—sometimes houses sell so quickly that the seller has yet to find a new place to move into.
- **An appraisal gap guarantee.** You can promise to bring the difference to the closing if the appraisal comes in low. Then your seller has one less thing that could cause the property to fall out of contract. They don't want to start over from square one either. (This is not our favorite option, as we already noted. You're effectively starting off with negative equity, and you'll need to see appreciation in order to break even.)
- **An inspection contingency.** By no means are we saying you shouldn't get an inspection. (*Always* get an inspection.) Instead, you can make it clear to the seller that you're not going to nitpick over everything in order to negotiate further on price. Essentially, you aren't going to ask for repairs on the "little things" in the inspection report. If you're only getting an inspection to check the major items—like the HVAC system, roof, structural integrity, and radon levels—make sure to note this in your offer and specify what needs to pass inspection. This contingency is especially helpful if you're buying an old, ugly home to force appreciation. You probably don't

care if the ancient shag carpet has stains on it when you're planning on ripping it all out anyway.

- **Show that you can close.** All concessions aside, the easiest thing you can do to make your offer more competitive is to prove to the seller that you can close. If you've followed our advice so far—you're a pre-approved, well-qualified borrower with a stable job and a ready down payment—you're showing the seller that you're financially awesome.

By adding any of these options to your offer contract (as well as demonstrating that you can close), you're tempting the seller to choose you over anyone else. If you love the house and know it's a good deal, one of these buyer concessions could make all the difference between going under contract or starting again from scratch. Still, make sure you're willing and able to offer each of these before you actually do—for example, don't opt for an appraisal gap guarantee if you're unable to bring extra cash to the closing. You'll be contractually obligated to do so should that issue arise.

# CHAPTER SUMMARY

- Your offer contract will dictate all the terms of the transaction, and it should be as specific as possible to avoid any confusion down the line. Your agent knows how to put it all together, but you should tell them to include anything that's important to you.
- There are about a million sections in your contract, but the most important are the purchase price, deadlines, inclusions and exclusions, and contingencies with which you can back out of the contract. Okay, we don't mean to pick favorites—*all* of them are important, but you should keep a special eye on these four.
- If you want your offer to be more competitive, you can up the purchase price, offer to pay some of the seller's fees and closing costs, or sweeten the deal with some of the non-monetary tactics we mentioned. Whether you need to up your game depends on how busy the market is and how much competition you have on this particular property, which your agent can gauge by asking the listing agent.
- Read your contract. Yes, all of it. This is a *little* more important than the checkbox agreement to download Candy Crush from the app store.

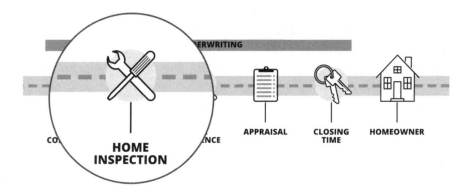

CHAPTER ELEVEN

# THE HOME INSPECTION

Ah, the home inspection—easily the scariest part of the home-buying process. It will be the subject of your nightmares. It will keep you up at night like a horror movie. (Home inspection. Home inspection. If you say it three times in the mirror, a certified inspector will appear behind you. Ah!)

This part is so important, we gave it its very own chapter.

A home inspection is a review of the property that gives you a snapshot of the physical condition the home is in at the time of inspection. Though it's not a guarantee that the home will be in pristine condition multiple years after purchase, it will tell you how everything appears to be functioning at the time of the inspection.

Here's how this process works: You make an offer on a house, and the offer is accepted. You go under contract. You celebrate. Then you have a limited amount of time to execute a home inspection and raise any objections about the current state of things. Based on your objections, the seller can either adjust their offer or hold their ground, in which case you need to decide whether the house's problems are worth the current price.

The reason the inspection is the Freddy Krueger of the home-buying process is because it's the biggest question mark you'll encounter on your journey—and it happens after you're already committed (and probably emotionally attached) to one house. Best-case scenario, the inspection will come back clean as a whistle. (Spoiler alert: We've never seen this happen in our thirty-plus years of buying and selling houses.) Medium-case scenario, there are a few small issues, but nothing big enough to lose sleep over. Worst-case scenario, big-ticket items like a bad electrical system, a plumbing issue, or structural problems can completely make or break your transaction.

Home inspections aren't cheap, and the buyer usually funds them unless otherwise stated in the contract. They are at least $400 but usually more, especially if you're adding on anything like radon testing or a sewer inspection. Yes, this is money that could go down the drain if you're forced to back out of the transaction. No, the seller won't reimburse you.

To which you might ask, "Do I *really* need a home inspection?"

Yes.

One more time, for the people in the back.

*Yes!*

Don't make us say it again, or so help us, we will turn this car around.

Though it is a $400–$600 gamble on a house you don't yet own, it's not as much of a gamble as forfeiting a home inspection and walking into a mysterious house that could fall apart at any minute. You need to know exactly what you're spending hundreds of thousands of dollars on. Big-ticket repairs cost much more than $600, and you want to know about any issues *before* you're committed to the place for five-plus years.

In case you're still skeptical, let's look at some typical prices of the Big Seven repairs. (Yes, we gave them their own name.)

- Foundation repair—starting at $10,000, but frequently much higher
- Roof replacement—starting at $6,000, but can be significantly more
- All-new plumbing system—starting at $10,000, but can be more. Are you sensing a theme here?
- Electrical rewiring—starting at $10,000
- Water damage—starting at $3,000
- Mold removal—starting at $3,000
- Termite damage—starting at $5,000

If your soul left your body for a minute, you can rein it back in by knowing that these can all be caught by a home inspection. Phew.

Once you go under contract, you should schedule a home inspection immediately so you don't miss your contractual deadlines. You can either go with your agent's recommendation or find your own inspection company by asking around and doing a little research. Either way, you should make sure you're getting a good home inspector. Make sure they have stellar reviews or at least come highly recommended from your agent, a friend, or a family member. You don't want to go the cheapest route possible—we love saving money too, but this just isn't worth it.

## What to Expect When You're Inspecting

Here's how it all goes down. The inspector arrives at the house, sets up any long-term tests (like radon, mold, or meth), and then starts the formal inspection. They will work from an extensive checklist so they don't miss anything, and they will take pictures to include in their report. They'll inspect every inch of the house, including the roof, either climbing up on it or using a fancy drone to take pictures of it. When the inspector is finished, they will walk the entire house again to show you, the buyer, everything they found during the inspection.

From start to finish, this entire process takes about four hours—excluding any long-term tests, which might need to be set up for days to get an accurate reading.

Though you don't need to be there for the entire four hours, you should be there for the last hour if at all possible. Why? If the inspector is as good as they should be, they're in multiple homes every week. Though your house is fresh in their mind while they're doing their job, it's not impossible that they'll forget it as soon as they walk out the door. They've seen so many houses that they all start to blur together, so the best time to ask your inspector for information about the house is while they're still in the house. And trust us, you'll want to ask a lot of questions.

Home inspectors have a knack for making trivial repairs seem huge and huge repairs seem trivial. If the inspector mentions something you aren't familiar with, consider asking, "Is that a ten-dollar fix or a ten-thousand-dollar fix?" While your inspector won't be able to provide you with an accurate repair quote, they can let you know if what you're looking at is an expensive fix or a manageable one.

As you're walking around the property, ask questions. And keep asking until you understand the answer. Like we said above, once that inspector is gone, they most likely won't remember the ins and outs of the home, so make sure all your questions are answered to your satisfaction on the spot.

Your final question to the inspector should be, "What is your opinion of the condition of this home? Would you let your mother buy it?" A good inspector won't hesitate to tell you their honest opinion. We've heard some astonishing stories of inspectors who look the buyer right in the eye and say, "Walk away from this house. It's a disaster." While you might not get such a direct response from your inspector, the tone and content of their reply might prove extremely valuable as you decide whether to continue the purchase process.

## WHAT'S NOT INCLUDED

The typical inspection will cover most aspects of your potential new home, but in most cases the inspector won't cover a few specialties—though some inspection companies will bundle these if you pay extra on top of your regular inspection. Whether you need to do any extra tests depends on the home, its age, and its location.

One to keep an eye on is the home's source of water. In desert areas, every home sold is required to include a Source of Water Addendum, which tells the buyer where their water comes from—usually from a well or the city. However, not all states have this requirement. If your state does not, you want to be sure you know where the water is coming from. If the source is a well, it's a great idea to have that well inspected.

Also, there are two ways to remove waste from a home: a hookup to a septic system or a hookup to the city sewer. (Or, as Mindy once had in a house she owned, a system that dumped directly into the crawl space beneath the home. Story for another time, maybe?)

Septic systems are more common in rural areas where access to city sewer and water isn't readily available. They need maintenance and care, and if you're considering purchasing a property with a septic system, we strongly encourage you to get a complete system inspection unless the sellers have done so within the last six to twelve months. While a complete inspection can be pricey, a new septic system can run into tens of thousands of dollars. Plus, some can't even be replaced—and a septic system is definitely not something you want to go without.

City sewer, however, is much more common, and it's serviced by the city in which the property is located. In most states, the homeowner is responsible for the sewer pipe that leads from the house to the main sewer line, which is typically (but not always) in the middle of the street. After that, any issues fall to the city.

For example, some older homes were built with clay pipes that can get crushed or shift and are easily infiltrated by tree roots. If you're held responsible for sewer issues in the future, that can be a $7,000-plus problem. During the inspection process, you will probably have to pay extra for a sewer inspection in order to gauge how your home's pipes are working.

While we recommend getting a sewer inspection, especially on an older home, the typical inspection could also reveal an absolute deal breaker before you even think about the sewer. Because sewer scopes cost an extra hundred dollars or so, you can wait to have it done until you are sure the regular inspection doesn't reveal anything that makes you walk away.

Radon, mold, asbestos, lead paint, meth, and even detailed fireplace, swimming pool, and pest inspections also vary on a case-by-case basis. Talk to your agent and inspector about whether you should go forward with any of these—and again, you can always wait until *after* the initial inspection is complete and clear of any red flags. Just make sure to complete all your inspections by the deadline in your contract.

## THE HOME INSPECTION REPORT

A day or two after your inspection, the inspector will send you a copy of your report.

Don't freak out. It's *huge*. We're talking 50 to 150 pages long. That's basically the same length as *The Great Gatsby*, but instead of flappers and emotional angst, you get to read about light switches and slow-draining sinks. As thrilling as that sounds, you should sit down, read the report, and take notes as you go. Share it with your agent if the inspector did not.

Nothing in the report should come as a shock, since you walked through everything with your inspector on-site. There will be endless small items that "need" to be fixed—meaning the inspector is required to call them out, but they won't actually make or break your transaction. We've never seen an inspection report where there wasn't at least one missing GFCI outlet near a water source (which is technically a safety hazard, but pretty common in a typical home). Smaller things like a leaky faucet, broken outlet, or faulty light switch are easy DIY fixes, or at least easy to hire out to a handyman.

There might be bigger issues in the report, though, to which you should pay close attention. Foundation work is expensive. Meth remediation is expensive, and mold remediation can be too. Electrical rewiring can run into the tens of thousands of dollars. Cast-iron pipes corrode from the inside out, so one day everything is fine, and the next morning there is raw sewage in your basement. But before we go there...

Stop. Take a breath. We're not trying to freak you out. If this is your first home purchase, you simply don't know what you don't know. That's why you're reading this book, after all—and that's exactly why we wrote it. We want you to buy a solid house, not a home that looks pretty but is on the verge of falling apart. If you're intentionally buying a house that needs work, we want you to understand the exact scope of that work.

In order to arm you with knowledge about each of these big-ticket repairs, we're going to have to scare you a little—but it comes from a place of love. Because the inspection report treats all problems equally, you need to know how to differentiate between a broken outlet and an entire electrical overhaul.

We talked about the Big Seven repairs (see, we knew that name would come in handy!) and what they might cost you. Let's talk a little bit more about what should be considered a deal breaker for a first-time home buyer.

## DON'T EVEN THINK ABOUT IT

- **Don't touch meth.** Probably good life advice in general, but we're talking about meth remediation. When a property is used to make meth, it becomes contaminated. Not only is it expensive to get cleaned, it's an obvious health and safety hazard. Unless your day job is working for a meth remediation firm, walk away from any home that tests positive for meth.
- **Significant foundation problems.** The foundation is the support structure of the entire home, so you can only imagine what happens if there are issues with it. Yes, these issues can be fixed—but they are extremely expensive and definitely not DIY.
- **Underground oil tanks.** Yes, this is a thing. Before anybody knew any better, they would use these buried tanks as a source of heating. Now these tanks are notorious for leaking and leaching chemicals

into the ground. Not only is it expensive to get one of these bad boys removed, but they are dangerous to you and the environment. And by expensive, we're talking $50,000-plus.

- **Knob-and-tube or aluminum wiring.** These electrical red flags are a blast from the past, and oftentimes insurance companies won't insure properties with these relics still in place. If you happen to be a licensed electrician, go for it. If you're not, this is a huge expense that you probably don't want to deal with.
- **Water damage.** The severity of the issue can vary, but bad water damage can signify structural problems, roof leaks, or plumbing issues—all of which you should avoid. Your home inspector can advise you on whether any water damage signifies a larger issue.

## EXERCISE CAUTION

Not every issue needs to be a deal breaker. Sometimes a lower price can be negotiated in exchange for taking care of a problem. (This also goes for the problems above, except meth. Just don't touch meth.) Here are some issues that you can overcome, but make sure you are aware of what you're getting into. Get multiple repair quotes before proceeding with your purchase, and definitely consider asking for a reduction of the home's price or a concession to cover the costs.

- **Mold.** These spores like to spread, and spread, and spread. However, some molds are worse than others. A mold test will determine what type (or types) of mold the home might have and what can be used to treat it. You can get rid of it, but it can be costly.
- **Radon.** This colorless, odorless, naturally occurring gas is difficult to pinpoint by location. While radon is more common in certain areas of the country, radon levels vary on a house-by-house basis. Your home can reveal off-the-charts radon levels, while your next-door neighbor has no radon at all. This can be remediated fairly easily and relatively inexpensively (closer to the $700–$1,200 range, which is not nearly as bad as some of the other things we've thrown at you). Your agent and home inspector can help you decide whether you should have a radon test performed.
- **Asbestos.** From the 1950s through the 1970s, asbestos was used in buildings because of its excellent insulation properties. Since then, asbestos has been proved to cause lung cancer, asbestosis,

and mesothelioma. It was banned from use in the late 1970s—but builders were allowed to use up their remaining supplies even after this date, so homes built into the 1980s can still contain this toxic material. (Whose brilliant idea was that?) The presence of asbestos is not an automatic deal breaker, since it can be remediated or encapsulated.

- **Roof damage.** Your inspector will call out even the smallest of dings on the roof, so you shouldn't be needlessly alarmed. However, if there are any leaks or major issues, you should proceed with caution. A typical asphalt shingle roof will last twenty-five to fifty years, and a replacement starts at $8,000 but can go up to $20,000 or more. (However, you may be able to negotiate with the seller to cover this cost through their home insurance. Talk with your agent about this option.)
- **Termites.** These wood-eating insects can cause significant damage to a property, essentially turning solid wood into a spongy mess. Though fixing termite damage is a big-ticket item, not everyone needs to be concerned. Termites are area-specific, so they may be less prevalent in some parts of the country. Here in Colorado, we see very few termites, so this is not part of our normal inspection process.
- **Lead paint.** Back in the day, lead was added to paint to help it dry quickly and resist moisture. What a brilliant, time-saving invention! Now we know that ingesting or inhaling even the smallest amount of lead paint can cause serious health problems. If built before 1978, your home is probably going to have lead paint somewhere inside, but it is likely covered up by multiple layers of non-lead paint. If this is the case, you should be concerned only if you're planning on disturbing the layers of paint by sanding or cutting into the walls.
- **HVAC.** This is a fancy acronym for heating, ventilation, and air-conditioning, so it includes your furnace, AC system, and the ducts throughout your home. A furnace will last up to twenty-five years and starts around $3,000. Whether or not air-conditioning is common depends on your area, but it is pricey to repair and even pricier to install if the home doesn't already have the ductwork in place.
- **Water heater.** A water heater will typically last about ten years and can cost $1,000 or more to replace, so you should be aware if it's near the end of its life span. This probably isn't a deal breaker, but you could try to get a seller concession to cover this cost in advance.

Frankly, it's impossible for us to review every potential inspection report scenario in this book. Talk to your agent about anything in your inspection report that seems confusing or scary. Talk to any friends or family members who are knowledgeable about construction or may have performed similar home repairs in the past. Confer with a specialist or handyman—but do it all very quickly with your inspection objection deadline in mind.

## HIRING TARGETED SPECIALISTS

Throughout your home inspection report, you will see comments that say something like, "Recommend contacting a licensed professional for further evaluation." Your inspector is able to call out that there *is* a problem, but because they're not a structural engineer, plumber, or electrician, they can't give you any professional advice within the report on how to *fix* the problem.

This is where attending the inspection comes in handy. You want to ask the inspector in person if they feel this is a serious issue. They are probably going to say, "I recommend contacting a licensed professional for further evaluation. But, in my opinion..." Sometimes they'll hint that it's not a big problem, but sometimes they'll emphasize that you should *really* get it checked out by a specialist.

While it can be difficult to spend *another* $600 on *another* inspection with *another* licensed professional, it is much worse to buy a home and discover an expensive problem. If you're willing to take on a home with any of the bigger problems listed above, you should have a specialist come in and evaluate the scope of the problem and estimate the cost of fixing it.

## I OBJECT!

Your contract will specify a fateful day by which you must submit an inspection objection notice to the seller in which you address any major issues found during the inspection. Usually, you either request that the seller make repairs to the home or provide a credit at closing to cover the cost of those repairs.

There is a lot of confusion among first-time home buyers regarding the home inspection and inspection report. Some people like to think that the seller will simply fix every issue that pops up. By no means are they required to accept your request, since this is one of those contractual checkpoints that works as an escape hatch for both buyer and seller. While the buyer can back out if they find a horrible case of mold/radon/asbestos in the basement, the seller can also refuse an overdone inspection objection.

Instead, ask your agent for guidance regarding what you should ask the seller to repair and what you should be prepared to handle yourself. No home is perfect, and you shouldn't expect yours to be either. The point of the inspection isn't to get a spotless home—the point is to not be surprised with a massive repair unless you're compensated with a price reduction.

Now that we've mentioned your two options—either the seller makes repairs or you get a credit at closing—you might be wondering which is the better choice. Though it may be tempting to request the repairs and get them off your hands, we actually recommend that you request a credit at closing.

"But then," you sigh, "I have to hire people and fix things."

True, it's a little more work. However, not only will the credit at closing reduce your total closing costs, but the seller is incentivized to have the repairs performed at the lowest possible price. They don't want to spend wads of cash on a repair for a home they're no longer going to live in, and you don't want to put the fate of your house (and your health, if we're talking about mold, asbestos, lead paint, or radon) in their hands. If you aren't comfortable with waiting for repairs—or if a repair is required for the sale to close per your lender—you can still work this into the inspection objection. Simply require the seller to use a certain company to perform the work, one that you've vetted on your own.

When putting together the inspection objection notice, make sure you and your agent are specific and direct. You don't want any ambiguity in your requests (and do remember that these are *requests*, since the seller can say no to any of them). You don't want to simply say something vague like, "Seller to clean gutters, cut down dead tree, and fix broken light switch in bedroom."

Instead, make sure everything is specified and numbered like so:

1. Seller to have gutters cleaned and all debris removed by June 14, 2021.
2. Seller to have dead tree on the eastern side of the front yard cut down and the wood hauled away by XYZ Tree Service no later than

June 14, 2021.

3. Seller to provide a credit at closing of $1,000 for missing GFCI outlets in kitchen and broken light switch in pink bedroom.

There is nothing ambiguous about these requests, and there's a specific date by which the work must be done. You want the report to leave absolutely nothing up to question. Though your agent should know to be as specific as possible, you should double-check their work when they send you the inspection objection for approval.

## R.E.S.P.E.C.T.

One time, a friend of ours was selling her house with a very long inspection deadline. The buyers had the inspection performed very early in the timeline, but they waited until the last minute before their deadline to drop the inspection objection notice on her. At the time, she was moving out of state and arranging a cross-country moving van, and she thought that since so much time had elapsed, they weren't going to ask for any repairs.

Instead, they submitted a massive list of repairs—and frankly, some of them were quite ridiculous—and demanded everything be done in two days. The seller felt bullied and intimidated.

Real estate transactions are often contentious, but they don't have to be. Other than the fact that the seller wants more money and you want to pay less of it (both of which are very reasonable desires), everyone is on the same page. They want to sell their house; you want to buy it. Both parties want the transaction to go as smoothly as possible.

If the inspection has revealed issues with the home, share the necessary repairs with the seller sooner rather than later. Some agents will say that holding off until the last minute uses the power of "negotiation" to your advantage, but we don't agree. Put yourself in the shoes of the other party and treat them with respect. This also goes for any other stage of the home-buying process—though the seller is opposite you in this transaction, they're still a human who wants to sell their house as quickly and smoothly as possible.

# WRAPPING IT ALL UP

The last step in the home inspection process is to submit the inspection objection notice to the seller before the deadline. As we've said many times before, you are making a *request*, not a demand—and the seller is under no obligation to comply with any or all of it. They can come back and say yes to some portions of your request and no to others, and you'll probably go back and forth with negotiations on certain requests that neither party wants to budge on.

At this point, you're incredibly attached to this house—you can try to stay aloof, but trust us, it's going to happen. You've jumped through hoops and spent time and money preparing to purchase this specific property. You're getting (or at least should be) a great price on a suitable home.

Determine what's important to you and what would make you walk away. While it may be tempting to throw in the towel with a few of your requests rather than give up on this house, you don't want to be stuck with a basement full of sewage unless you're fully prepared to wade through it (both metaphorically and literally).

If you are asking for no repairs or credits, you'll need to release the inspection contingency so you can move forward with the transaction. If the report has come back with deal breakers or the seller won't comprise, submit your Notice of Termination along with the Earnest Money Release form so you can receive your earnest money back and start your search again.

Sometimes, that's just the way the cookie crumbles. It's better to let the cookie crumble rather than the questionable foundation of your new home.

# CHAPTER SUMMARY

- Don't even ask if you need a home inspection. Unless you're ripping the home down to the studs—which is a very interesting choice for your first house—the answer is always yes. Yes, yes, and triple yes. Schedule your home inspection as soon as you go under contract, so you won't miss any of your deadlines.
- Make sure you show up for at least the last hour of your inspection so you're able to walk through the property with the inspector and ask any questions. It might sound unnecessary when you're about to get a tome of a report, but being there in person is a complete game changer. Don't be afraid to ask the inspector whether something is a ten-dollar or ten-thousand-dollar problem, and make sure you finish up by asking their opinion on the house overall.

- We recommend getting a sewer inspection, but you can do this after the initial inspection. Same goes for radon, mold, asbestos, lead paint, or pest inspections if you or your agent think any of them are necessary.
- If a potential property operates on a septic system or well water or is in a floodplain, proceed with a little extra caution. These aren't the kinds of problems you'll want to deal with in the future—at least, not without the proper preparation.
- Though the worst-case scenario of home inspections is straight out of a horror movie, it's more likely that your inspection report will come back with a mix of small and big problems (or, if you're really lucky, just small ones). Your agent can help you decide which smaller issues are too small to even bring up in the objection notice.
- With each objection, you can ask the seller to either fix the problem or issue a credit at closing. We recommend the latter, since you want your house, health, and safety in your own hands.
- As much as it sucks, don't be afraid to walk away if the inspection reveals something horrible or if the seller won't budge on any of your requests. You win some, you lose some.

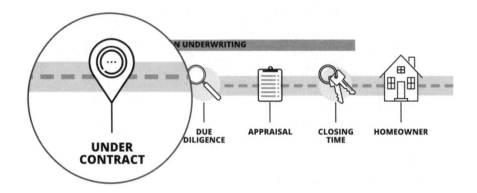

UNDERWRITING
DUE DILIGENCE
APPRAISAL
CLOSING TIME
HOMEOWNER
UNDER CONTRACT

CHAPTER TWELVE

# UNDER CONTRACT

Let's pretend for a minute that we didn't just spend an entire chapter scaring you about your home inspection. Rewind a few pages to where you are making an offer on a home you like.

If you're in a seller's market, you've probably made a couple of offers already. Those offers were rejected. You got your hopes up, and they came crashing back down. And just when you're thinking you read an entire book about buying a house for nothing—and those crazy authors had *no* idea what they were talking about—you get a call from your agent.

*Must be another rejection,* you think. It's like being picked for a dodge-ball team all over again. You pretended you were fine with being picked last back then, and you will pretend you're fine with it now.

Instead, your agent tells you that your offer was accepted. You can hardly believe your ears.

You are now—drumroll—under contract!

Your agent will guide you through this entire process, so there's no need to be intimidated. You should, however, be proactively informed about all the steps you will encounter. Everything needs to be completed within a fairly short time frame—usually only thirty to forty-five days from this point to closing—which means there's little time to waste during the process.

Because there are so many steps involved, here's an overview of what you'll do from contract to closing, all of which we'll cover in this chapter:

- Let your lender know you're under contract
- Schedule an inspection
- Keep track of your dates
- Read HOA documents (if applicable)
- Deposit earnest money (safely)
- Choose an insurance company
- Perform due diligence
- Check for permits and perform a title check
- Go through loan underwriting and lock in your interest rate
- Understand the appraisal process
- Close on your new home!

## FIRST THINGS FIRST

The very first order of business is to let your lender know you're under contract. Double-check that your lender has all the documents they need, and if they're missing anything, get it to them as soon as possible. Your financial fate is in their hands.

If you didn't contact a home inspector when you made the offer, that's step number two. Schedule the home inspection as soon as possible, and make plans to be there so you can talk to the inspector. Your agent should be able to recommend a good inspector.

Read any HOA documents, if applicable. The HOA covenants, conditions, and restrictions (CCRs) are the rules that govern the community. These can usually be found by searching online for the name of the neighborhood, the city in which it is located, and the term "HOA." The only time you can object to these rules is *before* you purchase the home, and the only way to object is to not buy the home. Once you buy a house in the neighborhood, you are required to follow those rules, no questions asked.

Most CCRs are dozens of pages long. They are dry. They are boring. But you need to know what's in there. Not only do the documents detail the rules, they also detail the remedies, including fines and even litigation. Read them in advance to make sure you actually want to be bound by them. This should be one of the first things you do because it costs nothing, and if you find rules you disagree with, you want to do so before paying for a home inspection or appraisal.

If the CCRs are acceptable, check out the health of the HOA itself. What do the financials look like? How much money are they collecting, and how much of it is going into an account to pay for future common-area repairs? What is their current amount of reserves, when was their last major expenditure, and what is the next planned repair? One of the main benefits of an HOA is that they use your fees to maintain common areas, so you want to make sure they're actually going to do what they say they will.

Finally, before you move on to anything else in the process, sit down with your trusty calendar and enter every date and deadline from the contract. Consider entering these dates one day in advance. You do not want to miss a deadline—it's a very silly reason to fall out of contract or lose your earnest money.

# EARNEST MONEY AND WIRE FRAUD

Another early step is to contact your title company for instructions on how to deposit your earnest money, since this is one of the earliest deadlines you must meet. As the buyer, you will most likely use a wire transfer to send your down payment to the title company. Cashier's checks used to be accepted but have become too easy to fake, so many closing companies only allow wire transfers.

Along with any extra money due at closing, earnest money is the biggest chunk of change you will put toward your home. If you've never sent more than $5,000 electronically to someone else, put on some deodorant, get ready to sweat a little, and please read this next section carefully.

Unfortunately, wire fraud has recently taken the real estate industry by storm. It is a very real and devastating problem. The scammer hacks into the email account of someone who is involved in a real estate transaction (or creates an almost identical account) and contacts the buyer, telling them that the bank account routing information they were given was incorrect. Here's the new info, send me my money, and have a nice day.

The buyer then changes their wire instructions and the money is sent to the scammer—and lost forever. We're talking tens or even hundreds of thousands of dollars. Poof! Gone. Irretrievable.

Here's the skinny, and pay close attention:

- Your title/closing company will not change their wire instructions at the last minute.
- Your title/closing company will not accidentally give you the wrong instructions and then need to change them.
- Your title/closing company will not email you wire instructions— unless they do so through an encrypted email. And even then, the instructions will match what you learned in person from the title company.
- Your real estate agent has nothing to do with your title company, deposit, down payment, or wire transfer. He or she will not send you updated wire instructions.
- *No one* is sending this information at 2 a.m., so check the time the email was sent.

When you drop off the earnest money check at the title company, ask for a copy of their wire instructions for the down payment. (You'll receive a piece of paper with everything printed out.) Once you receive the instructions, ask whether they'll ever change. They won't. So don't send money anywhere but to the account listed on that page. Ever.

# CHOOSING AN INSURANCE COMPANY

In order to close on your loan, you will need to commit to a homeowner's insurance policy. As we mentioned before, your lender requires the home to be covered by insurance, so there's no getting out of this one.

Your lender or agent might recommend some insurance providers, but you aren't required to use any of them. It's a good idea to reach out to these providers and a few more to compare rates. Each company will ask for information like your closing date, the square footage of the house, the age of the home's roof, whether there's a finished or unfinished basement, and so on. They might also offer to bundle your auto and/or life insurance with your policy, which can be a great deal—just double-check the numbers against what you currently pay before committing.

Each company will provide an insurance quote, which details the overall cost—usually one big amount that covers the entire year. Though the numbers here are important, you should also keep an eye on each policy's coverage, since some might offer more features or lower deductibles. If you're not sure what is or isn't covered, don't be afraid to ask the insurance agent who gave you the quote. They should be able to describe what each item on the quote means in a straightforward way. If not, they might not be your best option.

Just as you did when choosing a lender, you can make a list or spreadsheet with information from each company to compare apples to apples. This, however, isn't as big or scary a commitment. If you don't like your insurance policy, you can always switch providers after the first year. You can also make changes to the policy itself, like adding a discount for which you qualify, within the first year.

When you choose your insurance provider, they'll want you to sign a document so they can bind your insurance. You can connect your lender and the insurance agent at this point, and they'll work out the necessary documentation prior to closing on the loan.

## DUE DILIGENCE

Performing due diligence means researching information about a property to determine whether you want to continue with the purchase. Basically, you're looking deeper into the property after your offer has been accepted to verify the information given to you by the seller, check the condition of the home, and look further into anything that is important to you.

When you're moving into a property, you'll be spending a lot of time there. There are tangible things to consider, like utility costs, structural integrity, and code compliance. There are also intangible things that might matter to you but not to the seller or another buyer—like neighbors, noise, and so on. You do not want to move in only to discover that the boy next door is a budding rock drummer who practices all day in his attic. (Best of luck, as that might be a very...drum-attic problem. *Ba-dum tss!*)

First off, you'll want to verify the information the seller has shared with you. Read through the Seller's Property Disclosure if you haven't already. Call up the HOA to determine that the amount due is what they're actually charging. Verify that it's due monthly, quarterly, or annually. One thousand dollars a quarter may be palatable; $1,000 a month may not.

This is also the time to request copies of utility bills and any instruction manuals for appliances and systems. If the age of anything is not noted in the seller's property disclosure statement, ask how old the appliances, systems, roof, windows, and siding are.

Here's another fun one: Google the address. Did your home make the news? Was there an event, positive or negative? (Scott once bought a fourplex in which a shooting had taken place. He bought it anyway, but at least he knew what he was getting into.)

## Pulling Permits

When anyone makes a major alteration to a house, they need to pull a permit. Which projects do and don't need a permit varies by city—but adding a structure, plumbing, or any electrical wiring will most likely require one.

However, rule breaking is not uncommon. Not everyone actually *gets* a permit, and this is where things get sticky. If the seller or any prior owner did work on the house without pulling a permit, the new owner will be responsible for getting it up to code. (Yep, that's you.) And not even the code that was applicable when the work was originally done, but the current code, which changes regularly and can vary widely from year to year.

If your city is very strict, that spells extra trouble. In one city just outside of Denver, it's extremely difficult to get permits and work approved, so people like to tiptoe around the rules. If they are caught, they are heavily fined—or in some extreme cases, they're required to remove the improvements and return the house to its previous condition.

Long story short, you must proceed with caution. Let's say your house is in a cookie-cutter 1950s neighborhood and every home on the block has the same exact layout. You notice in your research for comparable home prices that all the neighboring houses have a compartmentalized kitchen, but yours is wonderfully open to the living room. What a steal, right? Unless, that is, that DIY renovator didn't pull a permit or pass an inspection. In that case, knocking down walls for the custom "open concept" kitchen was a violation that you might have to pay to correct.

If you suspect there could have been work done on the home, call your city permit office and ask whether permits were pulled and a Certificate of Occupancy was issued—which means the renovations have passed all inspections. It might *look* like someone converted the detached garage into bedroom space, but it could be a sneaky addition that's about to become your headache.

## Title Check

Because "title" is the most vague and confusing thing you will encounter, let's go over the basics one more time. Title is an owner's legal interest in the home. During closing, there will be a title transfer in which you are granted ownership of the property. Title insurance protects both you and your lender from any defects in the title, which could arise if there is anything that gives another party a claim to the property.

Your title commitment—basically, a breakdown of your title insurance policy—will be sent within ten days of going under contract. You most likely have a deadline for receiving this and canceling if you don't like what you see.

Title is massively complex, and each property is different. We're not going to pretend to understand all the intricacies of title insurance. The title company will assign a representative to handle your file, and this is the person you should ask all your questions about the title policy.

Your title insurance commitment will list what your title policy will not cover. There are preprinted general exceptions that are not covered across the board, like water rights, Native American treaty rights, and taxes that are not yet payable. You should read this preprinted section, but that's not what's most important.

You're more concerned with the special exceptions. These are specific to the property you are purchasing. Most common are utility easements, taxes that have been assessed, and HOA CCRs. Read this section carefully. Much of it will make sense, but some exceptions can be very confusing. If there's anything you don't understand, you need to call the title representative and ask them to explain.

Genuine title problems can be a huge legal headache, and they take a long, long time to rectify. This is a very important part of your due diligence—you should understand exactly what is and is not being insured before you buy the home.

# THE LOAN PROCESS

Though you've already done a lot of work to get preapproved, the loan process doesn't actually start until you are under contract on a property. Now that things are official, your loan will be underwritten—basically, a team of people working for your lender will look into your finances and prospective property and decide if they will extend a loan. Your offer contract should have stated a deadline by which you must apply for the loan. Make sure you're working with your lender before this deadline passes, or you could be in breach of contract.

Remember, absolutely no financial monkey business is allowed until your loan closes. Every real estate agent has a horror story about that one client who charged a house full of furniture to their credit card two weeks before closing, resulting in the loss of the loan and the house falling out of contract.

Don't be that person.

Financial monkey business includes but is not limited to:

1. Opening new lines of credit (credit cards or loans of any type)
2. Buying a new car. Yes, cars die and need to be replaced, but hold off on buying one if humanly possible. Definitely check in with your lender if you *must* buy a new car before closing.
3. Changing jobs. It's best to stay where you are through the purchase process, so you'll just have to deal with Betty in Accounting for another few weeks or months before jumping ship.
4. Missing payments on anything, especially bills that get reported to credit bureaus.
5. In fact, the entire time you are looking for a house and going through the loan process, try to spend as little as you can. Save the extra money for unexpected expenses during the transaction.

Okay, back to the lending process. You've sent in your documents and contract, and there's not a hint of financial monkey business to be seen. Underwriting will take the duration of the thirty- to forty-five-day contract window, and then your loan will either be approved, rejected, or approved with conditions—for example, pending the review of additional documents to explain some gaps in your application.

As underwriting is under way, your lender will also give you a call to ask about locking in your interest rate. Since mortgage rates can fluctuate on a daily basis, your lender will guarantee to lock your rate regardless of what the market is doing. Typically, a forty-five-day lock is recommended, unless you're fairly certain everyone will be ready to close on the house faster than that. You should follow your lender's advice on how long to lock and let them know about anything that could cause delays on your end.

Your lender can give solid advice on when to lock in your rate.

Depending on how your market is doing, it might be a no-brainer to lock in the rate right away (say, when rates are at an all-time low) or try to wait them out. Because of daily fluctuations, you can also try asking your lender to lock in the rate once it hits a certain number, so long as that number is reasonable.

You might be watching rates after you lock, and sometimes they just keep going down. That raises a common question: If interest rates drop, is there *any* way to get a lower rate? Different lenders have different policies. Most lenders will charge to break your rate lock (usually a set amount, like .05 percent of the loan), and some will offer to change the rate if it makes a drastic change. Make sure to ask your lender what their policies are before you lock in a rate.

## THE APPRAISAL

If you are using a mortgage to buy your home, your lender will require an appraisal, since they want to make sure your home is worth what you're paying or more. (How nice of them, right? Of course, it has *nothing* to do with the fact that the home acts as collateral in case you default on the loan.)

Typically, the lender will order the appraiser on their own, and you, the home buyer, are involved only at the very end, when the appraisal report comes in. The cost of the appraisal is often packaged up in your lender fees, so while you don't pay the appraiser, you are technically paying for the appraisal. This will be one of the last things in the purchase timeline, since you don't want to pay for an appraisal only to discover deal breakers in the home inspection or issues with loan qualification.

An appraisal is based on what similar properties in your area have sold for recently. Lots of ambiguity in that sentence, right? "Similar properties" and "in your area" and "recently": That leaves a lot of room for interpretation.

The number one rule of real estate is location, location, location. Because only one home exists in exactly the same location, there is never a duplicate for an easy comparison. The best anyone can do is compare the sold prices of "similar" homes, but even a similar property will not be identical. Even in a cookie-cutter subdivision, the same model will have different finishes—so "similar" is all we've got.

The appraiser will pull a list of homes within a half-mile radius that have sold in the last three to six months that have the same number of bedrooms and bathrooms as the home you're purchasing. If they don't get enough hits, they'll widen the search. What comes out of this is an apples-to-apples comparison—and even if the results are all different *types* of apples, they're similar enough to understand the value of your new home.

The appraiser will settle on a single number. That number determines your fate. If the appraised value of your home is *more* than the amount of your loan, you and your loan are safe. On the other hand, if the appraised value of your home is *less* than the amount of your loan, you might be in trouble. You have four options in order to proceed:

1. The seller can agree to reduce the purchase price, and you can make an amendment to the contract. This is the easiest solution but also the one sellers like least (for obvious reasons). If the appraisal comes in below your offer price, you should pursue this option first.

2. You can bring the difference to the table out of your own pocket so the loan amount does not exceed the home's value. Your lender won't allow you to finance the difference—you must pay in cash. If you still want the house and the seller won't drop the price, you'll have to pony up the difference at closing. (Note that this is not an option for VA loans.)

3. You can back out of the purchase entirely. If you have a home appraisal contingency, you are allowed to cancel the contract and get your earnest money back—so long as you and your agent fill out the proper forms and submit them before the deadline specified in your contract.

4. You can request a new appraisal. If you feel the appraiser made mistakes or did not perform the appraisal properly, check in with your lender to see whether they'd be willing to have another appraisal performed. Yes, you'll have to pay for this new one too. (Note that this is not an option for FHA or VA loans.)

The good news is that most properties meet their appraised value, especially if you're going into the purchase with an understanding of what a "good" deal really is. If you're taking our earlier advice, you're not going to make an offer that is any higher than the home's actual value, and you have already done work very similar to what an appraiser does. You and your agent have reviewed comparable properties before making your offer, almost like an unofficial mini-appraisal. It's the exception and not the rule when the appraisal causes a fuss, but it does happen from time to time.

## WHILE YOU WAIT

After you've submitted your inspection objection notice and delivered all the documents to your lender, there's a lot of hurry up and wait. While a lot needs to be done between now and closing, there's also a lot of downtime. It's the perfect opportunity to wring your hands and pace around the room, hoping everything goes well.

Make a point to check your email every day, at least three times a day, to make sure you're not missing something important in the purchase process. Keep your phone charged and check voicemail frequently so you don't miss any important requests from your lender. Check in with your lender once a week to make sure they're not waiting on something from you that you somehow missed.

Pack your stuff. It takes a lot longer than you think. Make an "Open First" box that contains a roll of toilet paper for each bathroom, a roll of paper towels, soap, shampoo, toothpaste and sheets for each bed. Buy a new lock for the front and back doors so you can install them after you close. Buy a bulk pack of 9-volt batteries so you can update the smoke detectors.

And then, you wait. Try not to pace a trail into the floor.

## CLOSING TIME!

Once you've made it through the home inspection, loan process, appraisal, and all your due diligence—you're about to buy a house!

About a week before closing, you should go ask your bank about their procedures for wiring funds. Every bank is different, and you want to give yours enough time to prepare and send the wire. Lack of preparation is not a good excuse for missing a contractual deadline.

Your lender will verify your employment at least once more before closing, so don't quit your job just yet. (Seriously, if you're looking for a new job, do not change employers before closing.)

Your lender may also run your credit again, to which we again say: *no financial monkey business.* No new car, no furniture, no engagement ring that you put on a credit card. Every single lender in America has a truckload of stories about that marginal borrower who did something silly right before closing and could no longer qualify for a loan. Every single lender. If you are thinking about buying anything other than gas or groceries during the time between contract signing and closing, talk to your lender first. (And yes, we realize this is now the third time we've said this. We hope it's starting to sink in just how important it is to not engage in financial monkey business before closing.)

At least three days before closing, you will receive your closing statement, which accounts for everything you'll be paying, what the seller is paying, and how much money you will need to bring to the closing. Review these dollar amounts and prepare any extra money that you need to bring to the table. Call up the lender if anything doesn't make sense—but nothing should be a surprise at this point.

Remember when you dropped off your earnest-money check at the title company and picked up a copy of the wire transfer information? This is when you use that paper. Physically go into your bank and tell them you need to wire funds for a real estate closing. (Make sure the funds are in your account and available for use, or you're in Trouble with a capital T!) Hand the wire transfer instructions to the bank, and they will take over. Ask when the wire will be initiated and when the title company should receive it, then reach out to the title company to make sure it did arrive.

Your closer, usually a title representative, will give you a time and date for the closing. Plan to be there fifteen minutes early, and make sure to bring a government-issued ID and any funds you did not wire. (Ask your closing representative if there is a limit on funds you can bring to closing with a cashier's check. There has been an uptick in cashier's check fraud, and many title companies have very low limits for check acceptance.)

Right before your closing time, your agent will schedule an hour or so for a final walk-through. Make sure they do this, since this is your last chance to check out the property. During this hour, you can make sure the sellers didn't do anything they weren't supposed to, like punch fresh holes in what are about to be your walls. Check for any inclusions or exclusions that were in your contract, and keep an eye out for any damage. Usually, everything is hunky-dory, but this is your opportunity to double-check that the seller isn't trying to run off with the washer and dryer they were supposed to leave behind.

Last but not least, start lifting weights with your dominant hand—because you're going to be signing your name, a lot. Closing takes between 60 and 120 minutes, which is filled to the brim with signing and initialing a stack of official documentation.

Once everything is signed, you will get a set of keys to the house. (Assuming, of course, your possession date and closing date are the same.) You're allowed a cheesy picture or two to celebrate your success—we won't judge. Hold those keys high and bare your goofiest, slap-happiest grin to the camera.

You are now a homeowner. Congratulations!

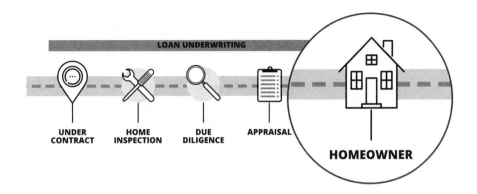

LOAN UNDERWRITING

UNDER
CONTRACT

HOME
INSPECTION

DUE
DILIGENCE

APPRAISAL

HOMEOWNER

CHAPTER THIRTEEN

# AFTER YOU CLOSE

Owning a first home is like learning how to swim. We would be remiss if we threw you into the pool without your arm floaties and left you there to fend for yourself. Once you sign all those papers, receive the keys to the house, and move in, you should be prepared for a few more things.

## YOUR FIRST STEPS AS A HOMEOWNER

Priority number one: *Celebrate!* After all that work, you deserve it. Get some sushi. Pop some champagne. Do whatever it is you like to do when you're feeling fancy. Because you *are* fancy—a fancy homeowner, that is!

At closing, you will receive a copy of all the documents you just signed, and some others will follow in the mail. One thing you might get at closing is a payment coupon for paying your mortgage when it is due. You will also get contact information and most likely a payment coupon for any future HOA dues. Don't lose these. If you do lose them or don't have them, contact your agent or lender and ask them for the appropriate payment information.

Your first mortgage payment is due whether or not the mortgage lender sends you a bill in the mail. The date of your first mortgage payment depends on the day you signed all the papers. Your closing rep should tell you if your first payment is due either on the first day of the month after closing or the first day of the *second* month after closing. Pay attention to this—you don't want to be late on your very first mortgage payment!

Any HOA dues are also payable without a mailed invoice. Your taxes and homeowner's insurance should also be wrapped into your mortgage payment, but make sure this is the case when you sign your documents. Reach out to your lender if you're at all confused about when and how to make this payment.

Some of your utilities might have been transferred to your name by the title company at closing, but make sure you take care of any leftovers. If you forget to pay your new electricity bill for a week, they'll give you a little leeway. A month—not so much. Make sure your water, electricity, trash removal, and Wi-Fi are ready to go. You might want to change your mailing address while you're at it.

Within the first few days of moving in, you're going to want to change the locks so you're the only one with keys to the castle. If you're hopeless with tools, that's okay—it's easy to hire a handyman for this. The same goes for the opener and code for your garage door, if you have one.

Make sure you add fresh batteries to your smoke alarms. If you don't have smoke alarms, you're going to want some. You should also consider picking up some carbon monoxide detectors and a fire extinguisher or two as well—you can never be too careful when it comes to the multi-hundred-thousand-dollar chunk of personal property that you now own.

# UPKEEP AND REPAIR

Even if you buy a brand-new home, something will break eventually. When we recently posed the question "What do you wish you knew before you bought your first house?" a fair number of people responded, "I wish I knew how much it would cost for upkeep and repairs."

One respondent had an excellent idea. She suggested putting 1 percent of the purchase price of the home into an account every year. If you have extra left over after repairs each year, the fund will just keep growing—and that's more financial security backing your home purchase.

Your main systems are going to be the most expensive to repair or replace, so those need your regular attention. A little goes a very long way.

Look at your furnace to see what size filter you need and buy twelve of them at a time. Replace the filter the day you move in, then mark that day on your calendar every month so you replace the filter regularly. If you have air-conditioning, this unit will be located outside the home. It has a protective grill surrounding the unit to keep the air intake material from being damaged. The air intake material will get clogged with random outside debris and should be vacuumed before you turn on the unit at the beginning of every season.

Your water heater will typically last eight to fifteen years. If your heater falls into this time frame when you buy the house, consider installing a water alarm near the base of the unit. The water heater fails from the inside out, and failure can start as a small leak. A water alarm can help you keep tabs on this.

If something ever goes horribly wrong and you find a high-dollar issue, always check to see whether your insurance policy covers that particular problem. While it doesn't normally cover poor home maintenance or neglect on your part, it might cover something out of your control—like damage caused by natural disasters or theft and vandalism. This varies from policy to policy, but it never hurts to check before doling out any cash.

Last but not least, anything from the inspection report that was not fixed by the seller should go on your to-do list. Keeping your home in good repair makes selling it much easier down the road. Years from now, you don't want those same issues popping up on the *next* buyer's inspection report.

# YOUR STUPID QUESTIONS, ANSWERED

Time for a classic philosophical question featured in many young classrooms: *Is there such a thing as a stupid question?* Your teacher's polite answer has always been and will always be "Of *course* not," and our answer is the same. If you've never bought a house before, even the smallest question can leave you wringing your hands for days—and Google doesn't always have the answers you need.

However, the stupidity of a question is based mainly on the sheer embarrassment felt while asking it. Have you ever had to pronounce "Worcestershire sauce" in front of someone from Massachusetts? Yeah, it's the same feeling as when you ask your lender if your new house comes with lightbulbs.

Don't worry, though—here's a long (and private) list of those painful new-homeowner questions you're too afraid to ask anyone else. And, of course, you should never be afraid to ask your agent or lender for clarification. They've heard it all before.

## Where do I start?

If you're confident that your financial situation is ready for homeownership, then the process starts with finding an agent and a lender. From there, you'll pursue loan preapproval, which will act as your ticket to making an offer on a house. (This is obviously an oversimplification. We did just write a whole book about this process, after all.)

## Can I actually afford the amount I'm preapproved for?

Technically, yes. Your lender wouldn't offer you a loan you can't afford; otherwise you would be a liability.

In our opinion, though, you should determine what you can afford prior to reaching out to lenders. Consider what you're willing to pay monthly toward housing, and factor that into your other monthly costs. We could write a whole separate book on personal finance (in fact, Scott already did—it's called *Set for Life*), but the gist is that you should consider your own comfort level more important than the number your lender gives you.

## As a married couple, is it better for just one or both of us to be on the loan?

There are many factors to consider, but the bottom line is that you can apply for more mortgages if you split up ownership—say, if you're interested in financing multiple properties with FHA loans. However, if something happens to one of the spouses, the remaining spouse may be required to refinance the loan or sell the property in the deceased spouse's name.

If you're unsure which option is better, talk to your lender during the preapproval process and they can break down what both options would look like. You might not be able to qualify for as much on one person's income, but it could be a better option if one person's credit score is lacking.

## How long does it take to buy a home?

Another huge oversimplification, but home shopping will take at least thirty to forty-five days and closing will take another thirty to forty-five days. However, don't limit your timeline for buying a house—refer to Chapter Five if you need a refresher on why this is a terrible idea.

## How does my agent get paid?

This is actually one of the most common first-time home buyer questions. A buyer's agent makes money by earning a commission of 2.5 to 3 percent of the property's purchase price. It's usually included in the seller's closing costs—meaning that you, the buyer, don't directly pay your agent. Of course, refer to your offer contract or ask your agent to confirm this.

## Should I get multiple home inspections to be safe?

Nope. Just make sure to hire a great inspector the first time around. The only time you should pursue extra inspections is when you need something not included with your typical home inspection (like a radon test, sewer scope, mold test, etc.)

## When am I allowed to back out of a contract and still keep my earnest money?

This depends on the "contingencies" section of your contract. Typically, the buyer is allowed to back out of a deal for four main reasons: the mortgage loan was not approved, problems came up with the home inspection, the appraised value of the home came in lower than the purchase price, or something fishy came up on the title. Again, check your contract or ask your agent for any clarification.

## If my earnest money is late, will I lose everything?

Technically, you can fall out of contract if you miss any of your deadlines. Best to make sure your earnest money gets into the hands of the title company before it's due. However, you wouldn't be asking this question if it weren't already a problem—so make sure to talk to your agent about the specifics of your contract. If the money is one or two days late, the seller *might* let it slide without causing a fuss. (They don't want to fall out of contract either.)

### I paid more in earnest money than the actual final closing costs. Do I get my money back?

First of all, you should celebrate your tiny victory! It's not the worst feeling in the world to get some money *back* when you buy a house. The answer here is yes—the title company is not allowed to keep your leftovers. They will send a refund check in the mail to cover the surplus, usually within a week or two of closing.

### Can the seller bail on our agreed price if the appraisal comes in much higher than I offered in the contract?

Definitely not. In the rare event that the appraisal comes in higher than the purchase price, the seller is contractually obligated to sell the house to you at the agreed-upon price, no matter what the appraisal says. They would be in breach of contract if they refuse to sell, and you may be able to sue for specific performance, which forces them to sell the house to you at that price. Plus, if they don't sell it to you, they can't go under contract with anyone else until your contract has ended—which you won't allow if you're trying to get the house.

### The previous owner changed something they weren't supposed to change (like taking shelves down and leaving a giant hole in the wall). Is this allowed?

Nope, unless otherwise specified in the contract. Removing anything that was attached is changing the home from the condition in which you saw it. If you notice something like this during your final walk-through, don't close until there is a satisfactory resolution. If this happens *after* your final walk-through (which would be unlikely and very sneaky on the seller's part), you can pursue legal action—or just choose to let it go. Some people are just bad apples.

### When do I get the keys?

You know how all your friends take a picture when they get their first set of keys? (Does the front of this book ring any bells?)

Most often, you'll get your house keys at closing, so long as your closing date and possession date are the same. You'll find all these deadlines in your offer contract. If the possession date isn't the same as the closing date, you will want to ask your agent when and where you can pick up the keys.

## So, does my house come with lightbulbs?

Or blinds? Or a shower curtain rod? Though big-ticket items like appliances are detailed in the inclusions and exclusions part of your contract, it doesn't exactly specify what will happen to the toilet paper.

The answer is maybe. Some sellers are generous, while others are absolutely stingy. We've seen sellers remove every lightbulb in the house—or, in one extreme instance, dig up every plant in the yard (only to be directed to replant everything, because that was a breach of contract).

A decent seller will make sure there is a roll of toilet paper on every spindle, a roll of paper towels in the kitchen, and at least one soap pump in the house. However, you should come prepared with a necessities box. Include all the good stuff—toilet paper, paper towels, soap, towels, a few glasses for drinking water, and all your caffeinated beverage necessities.

## How do I pay my mortgage?

Silly as it seems, this is another one of the most commonly asked questions by first-time home buyers. You close on the house, move in, and a few weeks later, you might be thinking to yourself, "Did I miss something? I don't remember how to make my payment."

Truth is, it's likely that no one directly told you *how* to do this, so you're not crazy. Before your first payment (the date of which will be specified in your loan documents), your lender should reach out to you with instructions. Most loan payments these days are made online.

If, for whatever reason, your lender doesn't reach out to you with payment instructions within the first month, feel free to reach out to them and ask about it. Just make sure you pay before the due date—being late with your first payment isn't exactly starting off on the right foot.

## What happens when my lender sells off my mortgage to someone else? Is anything going to change? Do I still contact my lender?

When your lender sells your mortgage to another servicer, the new company takes over. You don't need to contact the old lender any longer, and the new one will reach out to you in advance of your payment due date to let you know where to send the new payment.

Sometimes your lender will sell your loan but retain "servicing rights"—which means you still send payments to your initial lender, and they pass along those payments. In that case, you would still contact your initial lender with any questions.

## Why am I getting all this mail about my property after moving in? It looks like a scam—is it?

Here's something that very few people mention: You're going to get a lot of junk mail when you first move in. A *lot*. It's all going to look official, and some letters will ask you to make mysterious payments.

The thing is, your home purchase is public information. Anyone can see who purchased a home and when, and that information is commonly used to scam new homeowners into making petty payments. Some will look like tax, mortgage, or insurance information, and the scammer will ask you to pay a small fee to file something or sign up for something. The fee is so small that some people pay it just in case.

Open all this mail and read it. If it's from your lender—or whoever your lender sells your mortgage to—it's probably legitimate, but you can contact them and ask if you're not sure. If it's a notice that your lender sold your mortgage to XYZ Bank, make sure to verify this information before sending any payments to the new bank. (Heads up: It might not be a real bank.) Your initial lender will also send an email or contact you otherwise about selling your mortgage, so it shouldn't come totally out of the blue.

Long story short, don't send any payments in response to odd mail that you get at your new home. If you're unsure whether something is official, ask your lender or agent for guidance.

## What kind of tax benefits will I get as a homeowner?

One benefit we already talked about in Chapter Three relates to appreciation. As an individual homeowner, you can exclude up to $250,000 in capital gains from the sale of your home, or up to $500,000 on the sale of your home as a married couple. If you experience any sort of appreciation, you may not have to pay taxes on that gain when you sell your home. There is one catch: You usually must have lived in the property as a primary residence for two or more of the last five years.

Another benefit is the mortgage interest deduction. If you choose to itemize your tax deductions rather than using the standard deduction, you can reduce your taxable income by the amount of money you've paid in mortgage interest during the year. (Note that this applies only to mortgage *interest*, not the entire mortgage payment.) This is applicable to only the first $750,000 of your mortgage on the new home—meaning that if your loan is more than that, the excess interest deduction may be limited.

Your lender will send Form 1098 in January or February, which will include all the details should you choose to itemize this expense.

# A SMART HOME PURCHASE

To wrap everything up, let's pretend that Alex and Shelby from the introduction didn't make the standard American home purchase—instead, they educated themselves on smart home-buying strategies and made all the right choices along the way. Instead of their constant struggle after buying that $485,000 home, their journey would look a little more like this:

To start, they sit down and have a conversation about whether buying a home is really in their best interest. Setting all dreams and ego aside, they compare buying a home with their current apartment lifestyle. Because they plan on staying in the home for more than six years, they decide that homeownership is their best option. They are willing to recognize that buying a home isn't an "investment," but it is a better long-term option than renting in their scenario.

Before searching for a lender or agent, they spend some time analyzing their finances. They decide that they're willing to spend $2,200 on their total monthly mortgage payment (including principal, interest, taxes, and insurance), and they're prepared for the extra cost of any maintenance issues that arise.

They both have a credit score above 700, stable jobs, and a debt-to-income ratio below 45 percent. Collectively, they have $40,000 cash on hand for the down payment and closing costs. Because they want to reserve $10,000 in leftover funds after the purchase, they're going to use only $30,000 of that money toward the home purchase—which means they will almost definitely need to pay private mortgage insurance along with their monthly payment.

Shelby runs the numbers, and their maximum home price looks to be about $360,000. With a thirty-year fixed-rate loan at that price, they will be paying around $1,900 per month in PITI, plus $300 in PMI—which comes out to their maximum $2,200 monthly mortgage payment.

Even before they start looking at homes in earnest, Alex begins browsing listing sites like Zillow and Redfin to see what houses in their price range might look like. The type of house they want—a three-bedroom, two-bathroom home with a two-car garage and small yard—is reasonably available within their price range, and some of the homes even have updated kitchens and master suites like they've always wanted!

Nothing comparable in their favorite neighborhood has ever sold for that price, so Alex starts exploring other options. There are adjacent areas that offer similar amenities, so they're willing to budge on their "dream neighborhood" for the sake of getting everything else they want while staying within their price range.

Shelby also does some research on their current market. The city they want to live in is seeing appreciation rates higher than the national average of 3.4 percent, with a strong indication that this growth will continue—which only solidifies their choice to buy a house rather than continuing to rent.

Although their current lease is up in three months, they contact their landlord and ask to go on a month-to-month lease, and the landlord happily agrees for a $250 per month increase in rent. While this feels like a lot of wasted money, Alex and Shelby know that it's 100 percent worth it not to rush this major life decision.

Now that everything is ready to go, they decide to divide and conquer—Alex looks for a real estate agent while Shelby searches for a lender. They both get multiple recommendations from family, friends, and online resources, and they vet each option to find the best of the best.

They tell their chosen lender they're willing to pay a maximum of $2,200 per month, including PITI and any private mortgage insurance that might come along with their lower down payment. The lender confirms that the maximum home price they will be able to afford for that amount is somewhere around $370,000. (This is a little more than they initially thought, since the lender offers stellar mortgage rates in comparison to the competition.) The couple sends all the necessary information, and they're preapproved for a $400,000 loan—but they know that they still won't surpass the $360,000 benchmark they set for themselves.

Their agent of choice is impressed by how willing and able they are to transact on a home, so she's happy to work with them even though it might take a bit more time than the typical transaction. She confirms that $360,000 is a great price for what they want, and she sets them up to receive listings from the MLS that meet their needs.

As listings pop up on the MLS, Alex and Shelby run the numbers for any house that piques their interest. Is it the priciest house in the neighborhood, or is it the "worst" house in the neighborhood? Is it primed to increase in value, through both market and forced appreciation? Can the property be turned into a cash-flowing rental should they choose to do so in the future? If a house doesn't meet all these needs, that's not necessarily a deal breaker, but it is a piece of information that the couple factors into their decision-making process.

After a few weeks of viewing homes, they finally find one suitable enough to make an offer. That offer isn't accepted, but they don't give up. After making two more offers on homes that meet their needs, they finally go under contract! It's a three-bedroom, two-bathroom home in one of their preferred neighborhoods with an updated kitchen and a two-car garage, all for the offer price of $350,000 (which is $10,000 less than their maximum price, thanks to their agent's great advice).

They let their lender know they're under contract, give their earnest money to the title company, and set up a home inspection for the following week. Though the inspector makes it sound like everything is wrong with the home, his overall opinion is that the house is in good condition—except for the very old roof. Alex and Shelby decide to include the cost of roof repairs in their inspection objection notice, and after some negotiating, the seller agrees to give them a credit at closing to cover the costs.

Everything else happens in a blur: They perform all their due diligence, check for any clouds on the title, and choose a home insurance company. The appraisal comes back right at their $350,000 asking price. They lock in their interest rate with their lender, and the loan is finalized. Before Alex and Shelby know it, they are sitting at the title company with pens in hand. An hour of signatures later, they are proud homeowners!

As time goes on, the couple makes their $2,200 monthly payments with ease, and as they predicted, there's plenty of money to cover all costs while still building their savings and retirement accounts. They use the cash they received at closing to pay for a new roof. Their $10,000 cushion gives them a sense of security, and they even have to dip into it when a small problem arises with their house's plumbing—but when all is said and done, Alex and Shelby are completely financially secure.

Six years down the road, Alex and Shelby decide it's time to move into a bigger place. Not only has their home appreciated due to a steady increase in home prices in their neighborhood, but they added value by updating the kitchen and landscaping. They're sitting on a huge chunk of appreciation—enough to offset the transaction costs of buying and selling this house! Though they had plans to hang on to this home as a rental after moving out, they don't really need to take that route. Instead, they sell this home to move on to the next.

Their first home purchase served them well. Because of their brilliant preparation, there was no tossing and turning at night about their mortgage payments, no sense of desperation when that sewer expense popped up, and never a single concern that they wouldn't be able to afford their home. By resisting the allure of the American dream, Alex and Shelby gave up on the house on a hill and instead achieved something much, much greater: financial security, flexibility, and peace of mind.

Oh, and they were still able to give their dog a lovely yard and listen to Nickelback at full blast without anyone else's judgment. It's really a win-win for everyone.

# ADDENDUM

So, you made it to the end of this book. For that, we must congratulate you—by taking extra care to learn about the home-buying process, you are miles ahead of many of your peers. We hope this book made purchasing a home less financially and emotionally intimidating. If you can survive our bad puns, you can conquer the world!

Don't forget about all the free resources you can find at biggerpockets.com/homebuyerbonus. There's a rent-versus-buy analysis spreadsheet, a self-directed pre-inspection checklist, and all other sorts of bonus content that can help you on your home-buying journey. Always remember that you're not in this alone—and whether your questions are "stupid" or complex, feel free to ask for help in the BiggerPockets forums. There's a special thread dedicated to first-time home buyers at www.biggerpockets.com/FTHBforum.

Thank you for sticking with us until the end. Best of luck to you on this exciting adventure!

**P.S.** If you enjoyed this book, it would mean a lot to us if you would leave an honest review on Amazon. **Scan here to leave a review!**

# ACKNOWLEDGMENTS

The authors would like to heap praise and accolades on Kaylee Walterbach, the Publishing Marketing Coordinator here at BiggerPockets, an outstanding writer, and a recent first-time home buyer herself (as of summer 2020). When we first handed in our draft of this book, Kaylee immediately recognized the incongruity that our differing writing styles would bring. In many nights and long weekends, she heavily edited this book to bring one unified tone to its pages, and most of the incredible jokes and references found can be sourced to her creativity. Thank you, Kaylee! We could not have done it without your fabulous guidance.

Thank you also to Katie Miller, the head of our Publishing division at BiggerPockets, for her support throughout the writing and publication process. Her ability to put processes in place and logistical skills are unparalleled. We'd be remiss to not thank the entirety of the team at BiggerPockets for their support day in and day out to help our business achieve its goals and make real estate investing accessible to more people. Even more gratitude goes out to all of the editors and designers that made this book what it is: Louise Collazo for editing, Alicia Tatone for cover design, and Wendy Dunning for page design.

In addition to these key players, we would like to thank the hundreds of individuals we've interviewed on the *BiggerPockets Money Podcast*, the people we have met one-on-one for coffee or drinks, those who have been lucky enough to have been Mindy's clients, and the countless thousands of folks we've interacted with online through the BiggerPockets Forums and social media. Your collective input has helped frame our philosophy and approach to investing, real estate, home buying, and life in general.

Lastly, we'd like to thank our families. Scott's beautiful fiancé, Virginia, supported him with many early edits of the book and put up with many nights and weekends spend editing and refining its content. Scott would also like to thank his parents, Lynne and Randy, and his brother, Rusty, for their unwavering support through thick and thin.

Mindy would like to thank her husband, Carl, for his help with managing the day to day while she wrote this book, as well as her daughters Claire and Daphne for being cooperative and patient with dad's cooking during this time. Mindy would also like to thank her parents, Harry and Jacke, for helping her buy that first house that caused this real estate obsession.

# More from
# BiggerPockets Publishing

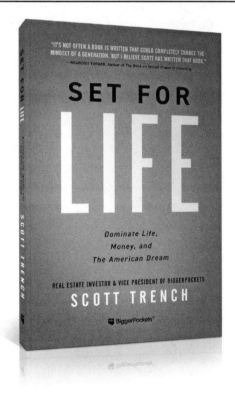

### *Set for Life: Dominate Life, Money, and the American Dream*

Looking for a plan to achieve financial freedom in just five to ten years? *Set for Life* by BiggerPockets CEO Scott Trench is a detailed fiscal plan targeted at the average-income earner starting with few or no assets. It will walk you through three stages of finance, guiding you to your first $25,000 in tangible net worth, then to your first $100,000, and then to financial freedom. *Set for Life* will teach you how to build a lifestyle, career, and investment portfolio capable of supporting financial freedom to let you live the life of your dreams.

If you enjoyed this book, we hope you'll take a moment to check out some of the other great material BiggerPockets offers. BiggerPockets is the real estate investing social network, marketplace, and information hub, designed to help make you a smarter real estate investor through podcasts, books, blog posts, videos, forums, and more. Sign up today—it's free! **Visit www.BiggerPockets.com.**

---

### *The House Hacking Strategy*

Don't pay for your home. Hack it and live for free! When mastered, house hacking can save you thousands of dollars in monthly expenses, build tens of thousands of dollars in equity each year, and provide the financial means to retire early. Discover why so many successful investors support their investment careers with house hacking—and learn from a frugality expert who has hacked his way toward financial freedom.

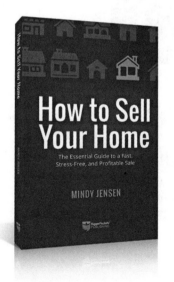

### *How to Sell Your Home*

Selling a home involves far more than sticking a "For Sale" sign in the yard. The stakes are much higher, since a single mistake can cost you thousands of dollars and months of stress. Author Mindy Jensen gives pages of practical, real-world advice to get your house sold for top dollar. Don't leave the biggest sale of your life to chance!

# More from BiggerPockets Publishing

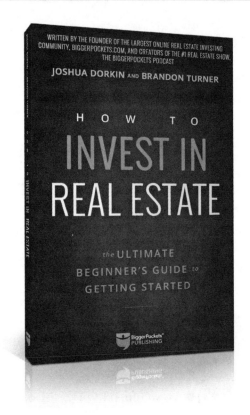

### *How to Invest in Real Estate*

Two of the biggest names in the real estate world teamed up to put together the most comprehensive manual ever written on getting started in the lucrative business of real estate investing. Joshua Dorkin and Brandon Turner give you an insider's look at the many different real estate niches and strategies so that you can find the one that works best for you, your resources, and your goals.

## The Book on Rental Property Investing

With nearly 400 pages of in-depth advice for building wealth through rental properties, this evergreen best seller imparts the practical and exciting strategies that investors across the world are using to build significant cash flow through real estate investing. Investor, best-selling author, and cohost of *The BiggerPockets Podcast* Brandon Turner has one goal in mind: to give you every strategy, tool, tip, and technique you need to become a millionaire rental property investor!

## The Book on Tax Strategies for the Savvy Real Estate Investor

Taxes! Boring and irritating, right? Perhaps. But if you want to succeed in real estate, your tax strategy will play a huge role in how fast you grow. A great tax strategy can save you thousands of dollars a year. A bad strategy could land you in legal trouble. With *The Book on Tax Strategies for the Savvy Real Estate Investor,* you'll find ways to deduct more, invest smarter, and pay far less to the IRS!

# CONNECT WITH BIGGERPOCKETS

## and Become Successful in Your Real Estate Business Today!

Facebook
/BiggerPockets

Instagram
@BiggerPockets

Twitter
@BiggerPockets

LinkedIn
/company/Bigger
Pockets

Website
BiggerPockets.com